Caring to Share: The Art of Selfless Giving

Rex Holiday et al.

Published by Rex Holiday, 2021.

CARING TO SHARE: THE ART OF SELFLESS GIVING

First edition. December 26, 2021.

ISBN: 979-8201031381

Written by Rex Holiday et al..

Table of Contents

Caring to Share:
The Art of Selfless Giving
by Rex Holiday, Summer Horenstein, and Steve Sonntag

Table of Contents

Acknowledgments by Rex Holiday

It is impossible to contribute to a book on caring and sharing without acknowledging the people in my life who have been my greatest source of inspiration on this topic. First, I have to give credit to my wife, Jane, who has taught me a great deal about what it means to serve other people without any expectation of reciprocation. My father, Charlie Holiday, was also a great example of selfless charity and service, and I am grateful for his example.

My great uncle Vernon Gordon was well known for his philanthropy and altruism with family, friends and even complete strangers. My sister Rita Holiday continues to devote her time and energy in giving back to the communities in which she lives.

I also want to give thanks to the late Steve Sonntag for inviting me to participate in another worthy book collaboration. Steve was another excellent example of someone who serves without any thought of reciprocation.

Of course, there are all of the benevolent and caring individuals who are featured in the interviews included in this book. We can learn a lot about philanthropy, altruism and caring from these exceptional people.

Finally, I give thanks to my Lord and Savior, Jesus Christ, without whom (knowing my nature) I would have no talent, no opportunity and no desire to care or share.

Acknowledgments by Summer Horenstein

Thank you readers for showing an interest in this book, and hopefully therefore an interest in caring and sharing.

I am so grateful for the opportunity I had to contribute to this project. I would like to thank Steve Sonntag and especially my father, Rex Holiday for inviting me on this venture, and for being patient with me through the process. Thank you to everyone who has contributed to this book in some way.

My gratitude extends also to the women in my life who have set the greatest examples of caring and sharing for me: my mother, Jane Holiday, and my grandmothers Lila Holiday and Diane Severinsen. These women have taught me lifelong lessons of selfless service, the power of kind words, the importance of being mindful of others, and the magic of having an open heart and home.

I am very blessed by and grateful for my loving husband, Phil, who is supportive and encouraging in all my endeavors. I would also like to thank my children who inspire me to become a better person.

Lastly, I am thankful for a loving God who has allowed us this mortal experience to challenge us and teach us to love one another as He loves us.

Acknowledgments by Steve Sonntag

I wish to dedicate *Caring to Share: How to Give to Others While Giving to Yourself* to my parents Lewis L. Sonntag and Natalie R. Sonntag, to my daughters Marissa Peterson and Sabrina Sonntag Canadell and their families, to the rest of my relatives, including my maternal grandmother Rebecca Yaspan who literally saved my life, gave me personal attention and love, and really was my mentor who originally inspired me to teach.

During my formative school years, my school counselor Mr. Osegueda, my Spanish teachers Mr. Harvey, Mrs. Cannon, and Dr. Galán, and the California State University International Program Director Dr. Lantos were particularly helpful and encouraging. It was because of their sincerity to students and their dedication to education that I also chose to become a teacher. Indeed, they were great role models for others as well for myself.

My fabulous personal friends, the Ballew family, Janice Lee Barsanti, Woody Brown, the DeGroot family, Miklos Fejer, Mike Forman, the Huang family, Arlene Krauss, Thu Lam, Aziza and Leo Mara, Michelle and Giovanna Mercurio, Christian Mitchell, Jordan Mitchell, the O'Leary family, the Ortiz-Wilson family, Karen Steves-Ott, Adele Stinson, Debbie Sugarman, the Vavra family, and the Williams family are very loving and very supportive people.

The Shalom-Nautico family has been an extremely important part of my personal life, and I am very thankful to have had them with me, as I have been with them. Jerry Hackett, who was a part of the Shalom-Nautico family with his philosophy of being self-full in order to become better personally, was very helpful for many of us, although he unfortunately passed.

My precious professional friends, Dr. Edward Brasmer, Marcia Chapman, Carol De Sá Campos, Mindie Dolson, Denise Elling, Sarah Fox, Jeff Gaines, Terri Godinez, Barbara Henry, Bill Jones, Joe Mora,

Nina Norton, Bonna Purdy, and Jim Stoker, have been exceptionally wonderful role models for so many people as well as for myself.

I also extend my professional acknowledgement to Bertram Linder, the educational literary agent, who originally guided me with my previous books for teachers and for families, although he unfortunately passed.

Along with all of my former students during my years of full-time teaching primarily at the awesome Manteca High School in Manteca, CA, I have had the pleasure in recent years of working with other great students, with their parents, and with adults who are also very inspirational, intelligent, and humble. Those particular students have been Allie, Alyssa, Amalea, Annie, Ashray, Bayan, Beau, Brooklyn, Claire, Connor, David, Davis, Dennis, Derek, Dylan, Enzo, Erfan, Erin, Grant, Haley, Hannah, Isabelle, Isis, Jessica, Jordan, Katie, Kim, Laura, Lauren, Leah, Leia, Lexy, Lydia, Manthi, Margaret, Marla, Matthew, Melissa, Miya, Natalie, Nicole, Patrick, Prisha, Rena, Ricky, Robert, Salima, Savannah, Sarah, Shaan, Shane, Sierriah, Sofia, Tiffany, Tim, and Yasmin.

Lastly, I wish to dedicate this book to my co-authors, Rex Holiday and Summer Horenstein who are very intelligent, very caring, very sincere, and very humble individuals. Thank you for joining me with this book! You are both awesome people!

To all of you whom I honor, thank you for being you! I admire all of you immensely!

Foreword

Perhaps the seasoned nonfiction writers and editors will find this entry to be a bit unconventional, but it is the result of an unconventional development during the process of writing and publishing this book. The honor of this section of a book is typically reserved for persons of notoriety on the topic or someone of an influential nature, celebrity status. How dare I, as one of this book's authors, presume that it would be appropriate for me to bestow upon myself this honor? Well, it is not myself that I hope to aggrandize, but the man who dared to dream up this book project. My words here are a memorial to the posthumous final author of this book.

Steve Sonntag was a man of great vision and I am honored that I was able to co-author two books with him. He spent all of his professional life teaching and for him every moment was a teaching moment. You only need to go to his social media accounts, that stand as lasting memorials to his legacy, to know just how much of an impact his life has had on his community and on the world. The prolific author he was, is in retrospect a blessing because we now have access to nearly a dozen of his works.

When Steve first approached me about writing this book, it was shortly after we had published our first collaborative work on education, and of course I was thrilled, but I was also curious about the topic. Why does he want to write a book about caring and sharing, and what does that have to do with education? Well, it wasn't long before I was able to make the connection because Steve took that as an opportunity to teach me what it means to really care enough to share.

As you read this book and progress through the chapters, you will be experiencing the work of Steve Sonntag in several manifestations. First, you will see how he so generously offered an opportunity to a novice author, as you read the first chapter written by Summer Horenstein in her nonfiction debut. Next, you will see how I had continued to be mentored by this great man. Finally, you will be able to read the words of the man himself, and those who were inspired by his type of benevolence in the words of fellow altruists.

Caring to Share: The Art of Selfless Giving is much more than a self-help or self-improvement book, but it is a look into the human soul through the eyes of its posthumous author, Steve Sonntag, and two of his writing proteges.

Introduction

In 2020 we were confronted with a global pandemic. It created many hardships for all of us, thus resulting in us needing to wash our hands much more frequently, not touching our faces, wearing masks and gloves, and social distancing. High risk groups were encouraged to remain in their homes. All of these measures were for ourselves and for others around us.

Many people began working in their homes as much as they could to continue earning a living as well. Essential workers worked incessant amounts of hours for the sake of the public, and they epitomized the roles of caregivers and people who share.

Another consequence was that many people became unemployed and filed for unemployment compensation; the pandemic had created a lot of emotional stress and financial hardships for them and for their loved ones.

Indeed, we all wished for the pandemic to end as quickly as possible. We became impatient, irritated, and concerned about family members and friends whom we hadn't seen for months. We were social animals who had mostly become isolated from one another.

Caring to Share: The Art of Selfless Giving emphasizes the importance of people helping others, essentially a great byproduct of the family basis of our society. Helpers need to authentically and generously care about people by helping them with their own resources as much as possible and, if need be, by referring them to whomever they know that will be of most benefit, if the caring people are unable to help the others well enough. This again needs to be done in moderation, because people who care and share have their own lives, too.

Caring To Share: The Art of Selfless Giving is thus worthy of your attention. It consists of Part I: The Ability To Care by Summer Horenstein, Part II: How To Share by Rex A. Holiday, Part III: The

Consequences and the Inspirations of Caring To Share by Steve Sonntag.

Each part of this book is very helpful. Each of us is inseparable and essential for a better world on a personal level, on a social level, on an academic level, and on a global level. Being a person who cares and shares creates a hero with uncommon courtesy, that is being aware of other people's situations and is willing to effectively and positively make a difference for others. Caring and sharing under our circumstances deserve to be considered that much more so, when it is possible and with moderation.

The authors of this book have interviewed various individuals, from Japan to Azerbaijan, from college students to a caregiver, all of whom have positively impacted their families, friends, and communities. We express our deepest gratitude to Anh, Jayne, Karen, Katie, Kory, Matthew, Miklos, Rita, Salima, Tara, and Tim for sharing their innermost thoughts and feelings for the benefit of you, our reader. They have responded to the following questions:

1. How has your past influenced you to do what you are doing or what you have done?
2. Is there anyone in the past and/or currently who has influenced you to be the caring, sharing kind of person who you are?
3. How have you been able to show that you care to share?
4. What have been the consequences of your ability to share? Will that experience influence your future decisions to share?
5. How have you been able to give to others while not overdoing it?
6. What advice would you give to others who will be reading this book so that they have a more fulfilling life of giving and caring for themselves and for others?

It is suggested that you, the reader, also think about these questions for yourself, seeing that you will be able to reflect on your own life on how you care to share.

We, the authors of this book, ultimately wish to inspire everyone to accept the reality of our competitive world enveloped with a crisis while fulfilling our basic need to be humane in our treatment with one another to care and to share for the sake of humankind today and in the years to come; indeed, an uncommon courtesy that deserves to be common by everyone as much as possible. Our lives transcend the boundaries that separate our countries. Lastly, while we as the authors of this book have different perspectives, we have the same goal to advance and to emphasize the importance of treating one another respectfully and compassionately.

Part I:

The Ability To Care

By

Summer Horenstein

Humanitarian, humane, what do you think of when you hear these words? Perhaps they conjure up synonyms in your mind such as charity or compassion. Yet another word, human, indeed the very root word of the first two carries with it a different connotation these days (i.e. "I'm only human"). However, shouldn't the derivatives of our own species name suggest that caring for others is at our core? Yet we cannot argue that all around the globe, hunger, poverty, violence, and injustice abound. So, are we naturally caring like the words humanitarian and humane might suggest or does being "human" give us the excuse to fail in this regard?

Anthropologist David Graeber argues that altruism, a caring and compassionate attitude, is, in fact, a natural human trait. He believes there exists ancient and modern evidence of how human beings look to fill the needs of others without demanding payment or even thanks. (Caring for Others is What Made our Species Unique by Samuel Veisserie Ph.D.; Psychology Today)

If caring comes naturally, how can we enhance this natural ability and ensure that it is the more frequent reaction to the challenges in society? This chapter will be discussing our natural ability to care, and how to nurture that ability.

Chapter 1: Nurturing Our Natural Ability to Care

We enter this world in a state where our survival is dependent upon the caregiving of others. Thankfully parents are wired to nurture and provide for their children. That natural concern comes in part from instinct, but also connection. Most parents can describe those first feelings of joy, love, concern, and anxiety that washed over them as their newborn child was placed in their arms. Amazingly those feelings are not privy to biological parents alone.

Parents who adopt experience similar feelings when a child enters their home. Furthermore, even when we are not directly responsible for the well-being of a child, as in legal guardianship, we may still feel a desire to ensure their safety and happiness.

Children, in turn, acting on their own instincts as well as mimicking what they have observed, display nurturing and caring skills from young ages. Many of us, no doubt, have seen a young child go to comfort someone who is crying, or make an unprompted gesture to share. Of course, we have seen the opposite as well. While caring no doubt is a natural reaction, it is not our only reaction to another's suffering. Often, we choose between acting out of compassion or apathy? How can we increase our odds of choosing compassion? How can we nurture a more caring attitude?

According to Dr. Lorenzo Cohen (Ph.D.) "Numerous studies reveal self-compassion is related to improved psychological well-being *and the ability to respond compassionately to others.* Self-compassion is not ego-centric or selfish as in "putting oneself first." Rather, *taking care of ourselves first enables us to effectively care for others.*" (Cohen. "Compassion: Learning to Care for Oneself and Others". www.huffpost.com[1] . March 11, 2014. https://www.huffpost.com/entry/compassion_b_4557312).

Thus, to increase our ability to care for others, we need to demonstrate self-care. It is like when we are instructed in an airplane

---

1.   http://www.huffpost.com

that in the case that oxygen masks are needed, secures yours first; if we fail to heed that we risk failing to save ourselves and those around us.

Self-care is doing what is necessary to monitor and maintain our physical, mental, and emotional health and well-being. This may include things such as getting adequate sleep, keeping a good hygiene routine, making nutritious food choices, and drinking enough water. It may also involve less obvious but still important activities such as getting fresh air, seeing a doctor, exercising, developing a talent, socializing with others, or pursuing a hobby.

Most of these things we naturally want to do, but the demands on our time from outside sources may distract us from attending to these good habits. Due to the pressures from our many roles some of us may forfeit sleep. Others opt for fast, convenient, processed foods because restraints on their time make cooking a fresh meal seem like too much of a hassle. Skipping a workout, passing up a chance to visit with friends, missing a doctor checkup the list goes on and on. As much sense as putting the oxygen mask on ourselves first makes, we fail to do it in many instances. If we are not healthy and happy, we find it more difficult to care for others.

As we make efforts to see to our own needs first, we will find we have the energy and capacity to help others. Self-doubt in our ability may still come into play, but honest introspection will allow us to analyze what resources and skills are within our ability to access as we turn our attention to caring for others. Ideally the first "others" we look to help is our family.

Just as caring for ourselves is vital, seeing to the needs of those immediately within our sphere of influence is important too. When we skip caring for our immediate loved ones, we damage those relationships most precious to us. We also weaken society. The family unit is an important unit of society.

Parents, children, in-laws, and other relatives are usually the first to be aware of the needs of a family member. Ideally, those relatives are in a position to help or get help for that individual. The following story illustrates very well how a tight-knit family can ease the burdens of loved ones in need:

When Jami's daughter was diagnosed with Cystic Fibrosis her world became a whirlwind. Jami was a full-time mom of three children, but now she had one child who desperately needed her full attention. There was so much to process mentally and emotionally, as well as things to learn about the diagnosis, doctor appointments to attend, and treatments to administer. Jami was blessed to have her family there for support and help.

Her mother especially was there for her. Jami's mother traveled to be close to Jami's family. Her mother devoted her time to babysitting the other children as Jami spent long hours in the hospital with her youngest. Jami's mom also provided emotional support as Jami adjusted to her new reality. Jami said of this experience, "Honestly I would have probably had a mental breakdown without my Mom's help and support. It would have taken me longer to cope and get back on my feet again."

A role model of caring, Mother Theresa said, "If you want to change the world go home and love your family." Truly if everyone took seriously their roles of daughter, son, sister, brother, mother, father, aunt, uncle, grandparent, or cousin...if they cherished their loved ones and sacrificed for their well being... we would see an end to so much suffering.

When we distance ourselves from our families, we weaken our ability to be first responders in their time of need. Worse though and too often the case is when we allow ourselves to be the cause of our own family's misfortune. When as a society we not only neglect our duty to care for our family but we abuse those relations, we hurt not only those individuals but we cripple society.

While the community can and should play an important role in the nurturing of others; no government program, no private industry, no prescription, no payout, can perfectly fix the problems that stem from the disintegration of the family unit. Consistent effort to love and support our immediate family members will be the greatest good we can do. However, even when we do this, we are not immune to the struggles of daily life. Sickness, unemployment, and the actions of those around us may place our families in greater need than we can manage alone. That is when we should look to our community.

The close quarters we keep in this world allow us to have some constant connection to the people around us, making it easier for us to reach out and ask for help from neighbors or government when the needs arise. We should remember to not only seek assistance from our neighbors but to give as well. We probably do not need to look far to find someone in need.

Start by becoming self-reliant and loving your family that already is so much, but know you can do more. You do not have to look far. Needs abound, and ways to help are all around. Consider your own individual talents, time, and resources. How can you help your community? Volunteer, donate, vote, attend, just be there and listen when you can. Act on impressions and never hesitate to do a good deed. The change may be imperceptible but your effort will make a difference for good.

Key Ideas to Remember:

- Take care of your own needs first in order to have greater capacity to help others.

- Maintain good family relationships so you can be a first responder in their time of need.

- When choosing a way to serve in your community consider what talents, skills, and resources you have to contribute.

Part II:

How to Share

By

Rex Holiday

Introduction

In Part II the process of sharing is explored in detail, including how a person can improve the ability to share, and what would happen if no one shared. In "The Irrepressible Instinct to Care and Share" chapter, the tone is set by examining whether *sharing* is a skill or an instinct, and some of the opinions of researchers on the topic of the nature of sharing are used to inspire reflection on the concept. This chapter also looks at what professionals and research experts say about the instinct to share; it is interesting to note that the experts do not all agree on why humans share.

Another interesting aspect of this section of the book is that we learn that according to some research it is by the same emotional instincts that drive us to have empathy and compassion for others that we also do unspeakable harm to others. It appears that choice is the thin line that divides compassion and cruelty.

The "The Making of a Philanthropist" chapter dares to challenge the philosophical and theoretical opinions set forth in the first chapter by implying that sharing can be a learned skill or at the very least people can improve their sharing skills. The chapter first explores perceptions of the *golden rule*, and particularly what is considered "golden" in the proverbial phrase. What exactly is *doing good*? Are acts of *doing good* the same for everyone?

Also, in the "The Making of a Philanthropist" chapter, the role of the philanthropic mentor and protégé is explored. There is a vast amount of knowledge to be gained from philanthropists, and the philanthropist protégé would not be considered successful until they put their skills to work.

The "Discovering the Giver in You" chapter sets forth the theory that sharing could be an art. Similar to learning philanthropy, individuals could be taught how to improve their sharing skills. For example, running is an instinct, but marathon runners and world class sprinters have taken that basic instinct to a much higher level. Just as these world class athletes train to increase their skills, the skill of *sharing* requires practice if it is going to be improved.

The "No Gift is More Precious than the One You *Give*" chapter explores the concept of giving without expecting something in return. The saying *paying it forward* has become synonymous to perpetuating the golden rule, but there is a healing power to serving others by sharing time, skills or other resources. In this same chapter there is a discussion on the concept of *inspiring others to serve* so that they too might discover the benefits of serving others.

The "No Gift is More Precious than the One You *Give*" chapter also explores how to turn those proverbial *lemons into lemonade*. It is probably safe to assume that most people become discouraged when faced with adversity or when that first attempt at some endeavor is not as successful as the expectation. The essence of this section of the chapter is to explain how to learn from those perceived failures.

Also, in the "No Gift is More Precious than the One You *Give*" chapter the concept of *when there is nothing left to give, just give time* is discussed. Caring and sharing should not create feelings of guilt, but instead should bring joy to the giver and the receiver; therefore, *when there is nothing left to give, just give time.* Finally, the "No Gift is More Precious than the One You *Give*" chapter explores *the healing power of serving when you are emotionally injured.* This section of the chapter sets forth the theory that the quickest way to find relief from emotional duress is by serving someone else.

In the "What If No One Knew How to Share?" chapter an allegory is presented to show the results of a world where no one knows how to share. The allegory demonstrates the present-day results and the historical implications of not sharing. Every technological innovation or scientific discovery that we are aware of and that we have benefitted from is the result of someone caring to share.

Chapter 2 - The Irrepressible Instinct to Care and Share

While for some people sharing is a major obstacle to their social development, it appears that from birth there is an inherent desire to share (Zaki, 2009). Furthermore, compassion has been observed in infants and toddlers (Seppälä, 2013). Beyond formal research studies that observe and analyze the psychosocial aspects of altruism, there are countless stories of people who spontaneously commit acts of kindness. From enemies on the battlefield to political opponents there is something that transcends philosophical differences when someone is in need of help.

There are historical examples of people who should be mortal enemies becoming inseparable friends. For example, during the 1973 robbery of the Sveriges Kreditbank in Stockholm, Sweden, the four hostages developed an irrational emotional attachment to their captors. A psychiatrist who had treated the hostages coined the phrase *Stockholm syndrome*. The term would become more widely used following the 1974 kidnapping of Patty Hearst (granddaughter of newspaper tycoon William Randolph Hearst) by the Symbionese Liberation Army (SLA), who, shortly after her capture, announced allegiance to the SLA.

Explanations for the Stockholm syndrome range from survival instinct to a sort of Oedipus complex where the hostages view their rescuers as enemies. While the many explanations of Stockholm syndrome certainly have professional and academic merit, few of these experts attribute the emotional condition called Stockholm syndrome to a possible human instinct to assume that there is some good in everyone. Stockholm syndrome does not only hint at an assumption of good in everyone, but an assumption that there is some common moral and emotional region in which mortal enemies can exist in harmony one with the other.

THE EMOTIONAL ASPECTS OF HUMAN INSTINCTS

In a research article on human instinct, emotion and thought, Levine (2017) argued that assuming that *reason* is always superior to *emotion* could lead to stereotyping people who are more prone to the emotional resolution of conflicts and challenges as weak-minded and irrational beings. We should be clear here that human emotions can certainly lead to some very irrational and even tragic consequences, but it would be naïve to believe that the latter are acts of weak-minded individuals. For example, some of the most notorious dictators in the last few centuries were undeniably driven by emotions, but many were also intellectual geniuses.

In their research study concerning pain, suffering and the brain, Devor, Rappaport and Rappaport (2015) discuss how the human instinct for empathy can cause loved ones to experience a sort of phantom pain when witnessing a loved one suffering real pain. Also, in their study, Devor, Rappaport and Rappaport explain how the instinct for empathy is so strong that some people will experience profound sorrow even when witnessing acts of cruelty inflicted upon an artificial intelligence (AI). Of course, there are also those who are less empathetic about the suffering of others as an AI.

Within human emotion, there appears to be an ongoing battle between the desire to do good to others and the desire to do others harm. The latter could be *harmful* in either a physical or emotional manifestation. A person who possesses exceptional strength could use that strength to assist those who lack physical prowess or they could use it to subdue their much weaker victim. Similarly, those with extraordinary intellects could use their genius to lead with integrity or to rule with treachery. Whether a person does good or harm to another person, ultimately comes down to choosing.

WHAT MAKES PEOPLE CHOOSE TO SHARE OR CARE?

There is hardly a person living who is not the recipient (directly or indirectly) of someone who chose to care enough to share their talents or resources to improve the human condition. It is easy to think of the

Newtons, Gutenbergs, Einsteins and Teslas, but what about the ones who gave us central heating and air conditioning, and running potable water? It is very easy to take for granted the things that we enjoy as a result of someone else's genius or generosity, and many of those who contributed to our luxuries did so knowing that they would receive very little or no recognition at all for their efforts.

Professor Thomas Widlok (2013) theorized that one reason why people share without expecting anything in return is that they perceive the thing that they are sharing to be more than what they require at the time of giving. Furthermore, the sharer takes no account for the value of the thing being shared, but only that it exceeds their own present needs. This type of sharing is perhaps more *philanthropic* than *benevolent*, and we will explore this concept in more detail in the next chapter ("The Making of a Philanthropist"). For now, we will explore further this question of what makes people share and care.

Going back to the example of our scientists and innovators who sacrificed most of their lives for the development of life changing technology, they did so because they experienced the same deprivation; living with a lack of clean running water, living in excessively hot climates or excessively cold climates. There are of course entrepreneurs who see monetary opportunities in providing that which can improve life for themselves and others, but even in those cases many times there is something more at the root of their motivation.

Never to be underestimated is *empathy* because it implies an emotional connection between two or more people, which is usually the result of sharing similar experiences of adversity. For example, there are several stories of how persons with perceived disabilities who manage to rise to the top of their field of expertise go on to inspire others with similar perceived disabilities. Two examples of the latter phenomena are professional surfer *Bethany Hamilton* and professional football player *Shaquem Griffin*; both inspired countless others to pursue what some may have considered to be impossible for someone with one arm or one hand.

Similarly, *compassion* is the ability to emotionally connect with those affected by adversity and those having adversative experiences. For example, some people can - without any feelings of obligation or guilt - pass by someone holding up a "Homeless Need Help" sign or someone stranded on the side of the road, while others find it emotionally and even physically difficult to do so. Why?

WHO BENEFITS THE MOST FROM CARING AND SHARING?

According to Laurie Cameron (2018), caregivers benefit from relieving the discomfort of their patients, and those who provide less relief care are more likely to have job related stress and burnout. Based on the latter research, it could be argued that caring for others is good for your health. In their research study on compassion-focused therapy (CFT), Leaviss and Uttley (2014) concluded that CFT showed promise as an intervention for mood disorders; originally a psychotherapeutic treatment for persons with mental health disorders pertaining to high shame and self-criticism. Caring for others could make you feel better about yourself.

The benefits of showing compassion through acts of caring and sharing are not limited to individuals. Researchers Friedman and Gerstein (2017) discovered that entire corporate organizations benefit from emphasizing compassion in their management style.

There is no need to comb through volumes of research studies to determine if one of the most motivating factors for wanting to share and care is the residual benefit the sharer and caregiver receives for their efforts. The simplest way to determine if there is validity to the research on caring and compassionate service, is to try it for yourself. There are many organizations and websites available to anyone looking for an opportunity to serve in their local communities. One such organization is JustServe (https://www.justserve.org/), but there are many more available by searching databases in your local library or on the Internet as will be noted in another chapter.

SUMMARY

Whether giving is motivated by a sense of duty or by a perception of an abundance and excess of means, it can lead to the improvement of emotional and mental health for the giver and the recipient. Praise and recognition is not always the motivation for acts of benevolence. Even when an expectation of reciprocation exists, it is not unreasonable to assume that there is something else in the psyche that drives desire to give. Whether instinct or moral compass, it more common for people to care about the well being of others, and for no reason other than it feels good to do so.

KEY IDEAS TO REMEMBER

- Regardless of what they might seem to be or what they have done, there is good to be found in everyone.

- Doing good or doing bad is ultimately a choice that people make.

- People show *empathy* to others because they are able to relate to another's adversity.

- People show *compassion* when they have developed the ability to set aside personal feelings or assumptions to help another.

- Individuals, communities and organizations can benefit from the emotional healing power of serving others.

Chapter 3 - No Gift is More Precious Than the One You Give

There are very few experiences as rewarding as seeing the smile of someone who has received a gift from you. Seeing that visual confirmation that your offering has been accepted with gratitude is an emotional triumph. One sure way to experience victory is to provide a gift of necessity to someone else. The recipient does not have to be an acquaintance of yours, and they do not have to know who you are in order for the experience to be special and memorable. In many ways, anonymous gift giving to strangers can be even more emotionally satisfying to the giver than personal gift giving.

One explanation for the preference to be anonymous might be the perception of low expectations for the gift recipient. If a recipient of the gift does not know you are going to give them a gift, then there is no need to meet their expectations. Also, in some cases the people you know might feel more empowered to complain or be dissatisfied with the gift that you give them because they know you on a personal level. Being anonymous in gift giving eliminates the emotional stress of meeting expectations.

PAYING IT FORWARD

As discussed in the chapter "The Makings of a Philanthropist" the concept of *paying it forward* implies an expression of gratitude for an act of selfless charity that has been received. In turn, the recipient of the charitable gesture performs an act of charity to someone else and so on it goes indefinitely. What if you have not received an act of charity to pay forward? What then?

How can you pay it forward if you do not have anything to pay forward? There are two answers to this latter question: 1) Paying it forward has to begin with someone, so it might as well begin with you. 2) Regardless of whether you have been the recipient of some act of charity, you have something to pay forward.

Never underestimate the value of experience, and life experiences are some of the most valued of all. Sharing knowledge is an excellent way to pay it forward and especially if the knowledge being shared has the ability to transform another person's life.

Teachers and mentors pay it forward by transferring knowledge to others that was transferred to them. In fact, formal teaching is probably the longest running string of pay it forward activity in the history of humankind. Since everyone possesses knowledge by education or experiences, everyone has something to do pay forward. Even bad experiences can be valuable resources when shared in the right situation.

LEMONS INTO LEMONADE

No doubt it is safe to say that no one welcomes tragedy, but unfortunately tragedy has a way of showing up uninvited. An interesting paradox of tragedy is that it can actually bring people together through mutual experiences.

Organizations such as Mothers Against Drunk Drivers (MADD) or the Polly Klass Foundation are the results of people using their traumatic life experiences to help others. It is much easier to wallow in self-pity than it is to turn tragedy into triumph. Those who find the courage and strength to help others by using what they have learned from personal adversity have the heart of a hero. Like the heroes of fiction, these true-life heroes inspire others to be like them.

INSPIRING OTHERS TO GIVE

Most people want to be happy and they want to see others happy too. If there is anything that nearly all charities have in common, is that they make people happy. Whether providing a meal or saving a life, charities have a way of putting a smile on the face of the recipient. When others observe something that is bringing joy to someone, they often want to be a part of that thing too, and not as the recipient.

Every act of kindness has the potential to inspire others to mimic that kindness. So then, the formula for inspiring others to give is to provide them with opportunities to see others giving and making people happy. The interesting thing about giving something good, is that you always receive something good in return.

THE HEALING POWER OF SERVING OTHERS WHEN YOU ARE EMOTIONALLY INJURED

Curwin (1993) explained how reward systems could be done away with when at-risk youth were allowed the opportunity to serve others who were in need. The emotional scars that contributed to those youth's at-risk behavior were healed through the acts of compassionate service that they gave. This is almost like the old technique of biting a bullet to misdirect the pain of having a bullet removed without anesthesia. When we are able to take our minds off of our own suffering by attending to the needs of others, we can experience some relief because our own problems are emotionally out of sight and out of mind.

Allan Luks (2004), a former executive director of the Institute for the Advancement of Health and executive director of Big Brothers/Big Sisters of New York City, conducted a study on the cause-and-effect relationship between helping and good health. The following are just a few of the results that Luks' research revealed about the relationship between helping and health:

- Helping others contributes to the maintenance of good health, and can reduce the effects of psychological and physical diseases.

- The health benefits return for hours or even days when the act of helping is remembered.

- Feelings of depression are reversed.

- The intensity of physical pain can decrease.

Based on these findings by Luks, it would seem that one method of healing our own mental, emotional or physical ailments is to help others to heal theirs.

Of course, it would be dishonest and misleading to imply that helping others is the cure for all ailments. It would also be misrepresenting to suggest that helping others first when you are physically or mentally impaired is always the right thing to do.

Sometimes it is better to attend to your own health first before you can effectively help another. Think of it as the airplane emergency oxygen principle, where you are instructed to place the oxygen over your own face first before you attempt to help anyone else to place the mask over their face. The simple logic behind this principle is that you cannot help someone else if you are unconscious from a lack of oxygen.

WHEN THERE IS NOTHING LEFT TO GIVE, JUST GIVE TIME

It is natural to associate the act of giving with a monetary investment, but giving does not have to involve money. The one thing that levels the playing field for every living human being is time. There are 24 hours in a day, and that is true for all people regardless of socioeconomic status. It is how we use our time that differentiates one person from another. It may seem that there is no choice in how you spend your time when it comes to career or other obligations, but there is always a choice. Even a person incarcerated and locked up in solitary confinement has a choice how they will spend their time.

For those of us who are free to come and go as they please, it is a good practice to review how we are using our precious valuable time each day. This is definitely a good-better-best principle because there are many efficient ways to spend out time above and beyond our daily work, school or guardian responsibilities. For example, it is good to take time to relax from a busy day at work or school, and engage in a pastime activity like reading, watching television or playing computer games.

It might be a better choice to spend that downtime acquiring a new skill that will help you to stay relevant in the professional arena. Exercising might also be a better choice.

Depending on individual perception and opinion, any of the pastime activities mentioned above could be time well spent. However, one of the best ways to spend spare time is by serving someone else, and this is specifically the kind of service that cost you nothing else but time.

There are many opportunities to serve others with your time, and we have already mentioned a few in earlier chapters. In addition to the nonprofit organizations, there are opportunities to serve a family member or a neighbor who is in need. Many senior living facilities welcome individuals who want to read to elderly residents or who might want to share a skill or a talent. The positive impact of serving others is immeasurable for the receiver and the giver.

SUMMARY

Giving anonymously can eliminate any expectations from the receiver but it can also eliminate the expectation of recognition from the giver. One of the most positive outcomes of giving is when others are inspired to give because they have received some act of kindness from another. Having the ability and the desire to turn a bad situation into an opportunity to help others is an excellent way to promote self-healing. Too often the concept of charity is tied to a monetary gift of gesture, but one of the most valuable things that a person can give to another is time. Some even say that another way to spell love is T-I-M-E.

KEY IDEAS TO REMEMBER

- Sharing knowledge is a great way to pay it forward.

- Most people want to be happy and they want to see others happy too.

● Sometimes it is better to attend to your own health first before you can effectively help another.

● It is how we use our time that differentiates one person from another.

Chapter 4 - The Makings of a Philanthropist

The benefits of philanthropy go deeper than charitable donations to the home of a successful person or entity. Tech startups rely on the investments of successful business entrepreneurs, and research scientists mostly rely on charitable foundations to fund their research projects. Breakthroughs in life improving technology and lifesaving science rely heavily philanthropic influences.

In the early days of Apple, Jobs and Wozniak had to rely on the philanthropy of investors like business entrepreneur Armas "Mike" Makkula to get their Apple II personal computer line up to market. Three decades later, Apple became synonymous with corporate success. In the summer of 2018 Apple became the first United States listed company to reach a stock-market value of one trillion dollars. Apple's phenomenal accomplishment was initially made possible by Makkula's $250,000 investment.

Are there other garage-bound computer engineers with ideas that could revolutionize technology who will never be discovered? That is a disturbingly valid question. It is quite possible that some of the best technological concepts – including those that improve or saves lives—will never be discovered for lack of philanthropic intervention.

What would happen if every multimillionaire or billionaire suddenly adopted a pay-it-forward philosophy? The outcome would be mixed for sure. In some instances, unfettered benevolence would nurture extraordinary results, but in other cases it could lead to mass corruption. There is no way to know for sure if an act of benevolence will yield positive results, but the potential benefits must surely outweigh the risks.

THE 'GOLD' IN THE GOLDEN RULE

Much like the storyline itself, when Catherine Ryan Hyde's novel *Pay it Forward* was released as a motion picture in 2000, a new concept of philanthropy was born. Fans of the novel were already familiar with the term, but after the release of the movie, the phrase "pay it forward" became the catchphrase for reciprocated benevolence. Suddenly people were impassioned by the idea that it was a moral obligation that anyone who was the recipient of benevolence seek out and execute an equal or even greater act of benevolence.

The golden rule states that a person should do to others as they would have others do to them. That could only mean that if we want the best *from* others, then we should always try to give our best *to* others. It is easy to justify holding back a little here and a little there, whether it be when we are donating time or material; the term *material* includes money. The question we should ask ourselves is "Am I holding back because I can't do more, or am I holding back because I won't do more?"

When giving to others, whether it is time or material, we should always make the best of every opportunity. There are two very good reasons for this approach to giving. The first reason is *no regrets*. For example, if there is an opportunity to serve someone in a way that will have a profound positive effect on their life, then that is definitely the time to give all that we can. Doing less will always leave us wondering if we could have done more.

The second reason to make the best of every opportunity to give, is to assure a *better outcome*. It is as simple as math because a half effort will undoubtedly yield a half result. Half efforts are always a waste of time, and not only for the person who is giving the half effort. This is particularly true when it comes to serving others. The time that you are taking to give what you know is not your best effort could be robbing someone else of an opportunity to give their best effort. Also, a half effort will rob the intended recipient of an opportunity to receive some else's best effort. The best rule when giving is to remember the *golden rule*.

THE PHILANTHROPIST MENTOR & PROTÉGÉ RELATIONSHIP

The last section was not meant to discourage you in anyway, but it was meant to inspire you to think of your true potential as a philanthropist. Afterall, the title of this chapter is "The Makings of a Philanthropist," which implies that you will have to start somewhere. As with any learned skill there is a teacher-student dynamic where knowledge is transferred from one who is more knowledgeable about a particular topic than another. However, in mentor-protégé relationships there is an implied more one-on-one interchange than what might occur in traditional teacher-student situations.

According to Haines (2003), mentoring is the primary way by which adults gain new knowledge. That would certainly seem to be true when given the fact that any type of training or education requires some form of a mentor-protégé relationship. College students and skilled labor apprentices have to rely on the knowledge of subject matter experts in order to obtain their ultimate career goals. The same is true of the relationship between the philanthropist and the aspiring philanthropist.

LEARNING FROM PHILANTHROPISTS

There is an unofficial rule in the dynamics of leadership, which dictates that all leaders lead by example. It is an inescapable fact that a bad leader leads by example just as much as a good leader leads by example. By the very definition of the word, a philanthropist is a good person at heart with good intentions. Similarly, most philanthropists by their very nature are leaders because they take the initiative to promote humanity.

There is a lot that an aspiring philanthropist can learn from watching and studying the actions and decisions of seasoned philanthropists. For one, it could be helpful to see what motivates a philanthropist to do the things that he or she does. Why do they give? Why do they give to a particular charity or individual? Learn what they are passionate about, and how they satisfy that passion.

Also, learn more about them as an individual, their background, beliefs, and any talents that they might possess. Some of these things might seem irrelevant, but you might find that the seemingly irrelevant things all lead to a pattern or a common denominator for all philanthropists.

USING WHAT YOU HAVE LEARNED FROM PHILANTHROPISTS

Knowledge is meant to be used and shared, so once you have had a chance to learn more about philanthropy, you should find opportunities to put into practice what you have learned. You can start small by seeking out local charities or looking for opportunities at the local schools in your community. Some excellent resources for aspiring philanthropists are websites like hungryformusic.org, nonprofitquarterly.org, philanthropyroundtable.org, and philanthropy.com. These sites provide opportunities to donate, volunteer, and learn more about philanthropy.

SUMMARY

The world certainly needs more philanthropists because the most successful charitable organizations benefit from the generosity of those who have substantial resources to donate. From cancer research to the distribution of medicine to impoverished communities plagued by disease, the philanthropic gestures of benevolent people of wealth has improved the world one donation or act of kindness at a time. It is not uncommon for those who have been blessed with much to be envied by those who have less, but it would be far more productive to mimic the habits of those with strong desires to share.

KEY IDEAS TO REMEMBER

- The benefits of benevolences outweigh any risks that the results might not be positive.

- Doing your best when serving others will mean fewer regrets in hindsight.

● Mentoring is the most common way that adults gain new knowledge.

● Look for opportunities to put into practice your new skills as a philanthropist

Chapter 5 - What if No One Knew How to Share?

It is doubtful that screenwriters Frances Goodrich and Albert Hackett or director Frank Capra could have imagined that their motion picture project would entertain several generations of fans. However, the theme of the Christmas movie "It's a Wonderful Life" prompts two of the oldest and most intriguing questions of human existence: *Who am I?* and *What is my purpose?*

While it is certainly tempting for this writer to launch into a philosophical and theological discussion, that is not the intent of this chapter. No, the goal here is to explore how our lives impact the world around us and how sharing inspires human progress.

WHAT IF SCENARIOS

Just as with the protagonist in Frank Capra's existential film, we sometimes lose our way and wonder if we are better off having never existed at all. However, just as with George Bailey, we all matter, and our lives impact other lives in ways that we cannot fully understand or even imagine. In the most subtle of ways one life touches another, and what at first appears to be an inconsequential contribution ends up being life changing. Furthermore, those life changing contributions made by one individual can change the world. The following *what-if* scenarios examine what might have happened if notable contributors didn't share.

ONCE UPON A TIME, THERE WERE TWO FRIENDS

A young man believed he had a good instinct for what was a viable business concept and he just couldn't see any value in his friend's computer concept. Afterall, IBM and Hewlett Packard had already cornered that market and they were giants in their own rights. Another thing that bothered the young man was that his friend had the foolish notion that his computer would catch on in the private sector. The computer geek friend actually believed people would purchase a computer to use for their own personal needs. *Poor fool*, the young man thought of his friend. *He's wasting his time and although we're friends, I can't afford to waste time with him.*

So, that young man with the gift for promoting creative concepts failed to see his friend's raw innovative insight and the two would be legends went their separate ways. Without the entrepreneurial genius of that young man, his computer geek friend lost interest in the personal computer concept and moved on to other less technologically revolutionary projects. Steve Jobs and Steve Wozniak never collaborate on the personal computer concept, so the Apple Computer 1 is never developed. Consequently, there is no such thing as iTunes, the Mac, iPod, iPad, iPhone, or Apple Watch.

A single choice could have prevented one of the greatest inventions since the internal combustion engine and air travel. Sure, it could be argued that if Jobs and Wozniak had not invented the Apple computer, then someone else would have eventually stumbled upon the technology. There is no way to know that for sure, but what we do know is that many of the things that are possible because of the personal computer may not have been accomplished without it. Wozniak didn't invent the computer, but he did inspire an entire computer industry. Jobs didn't live to Apple become a trillion-dollar company, but his contribution is undeniable.

THE EQUATION OF HIDDEN TALENTS

A young woman gets up from her desk, frustrated by how she has been treated by her male coworkers, and walks off the job, abandoning her dream of becoming an engineer. Another young woman decides that she has had enough of the policies of her employer that prevent her from realizing her true potential. A third woman merely glances at an ad for mathematicians at an aeronautical research facility before discarding it. The decisions of these three women have a trickle-down impact on a much larger project, and as a result, in the summer of 1969, the world watches in mesmerized curiosity, as Russian cosmonauts land on the moon.

Had Dorothy Vaughn, Mary Jackson, and Katherine Coleman Goble Johnson not cared enough to share their unique math talents, the outcome of the space race between the United States and Russia would have been in the latter's favor. The gifted women had to confront barriers that would have broken or discouraged most people, but they persevered and overcame those barriers. The entire world has benefitted from their perseverance, and decades later, United States astronauts and Russian cosmonauts work together to uncover the mysteries of space. That is despite ongoing political differences.

The previous scenarios are just fiction, but they cause us to explore some very uncomfortable possibilities. For example, how many life changing innovations never happened because someone decided that they did not want to share the limelight? How many times has the cure for cancer and other incurable diseases been delayed because those with the knowledge refused to come together in collaboration? Could a simple collaboration end the military conflicts that plague our planet? We will never know the answers to these questions but each of us can do our part to avoid being the one who did not share their gifts and talents.

THE IMPETUS OF COLLABORATION

When gifted and talented people work together towards a common goal, amazing things can happen. We have seen this time and time again in the fields of engineering and science. Caring to share is the impetus of collaboration, and many technological and scientific breakthroughs have been the results of collaboration. If we were to break through the barriers that impede creative alliances, the innovation of the human race would be limitless. However, that is much easier said than done because it is in our nature to pass judgement based on our perceptions, which only fortifies the barriers that impede our creative potential.

The collaboration of communities or entire nations often begin with an alliance between two people, and the positive influence that even a single person can have on the world is remarkable. We need only look at historical figures like Johannes Gutenberg (inventor of the printing press) to see how this is true, but even someone with far less ingenuity than Gutenberg can have a positive impact on the world. The communities in which we live are nothing more than tiny pieces of the world, so anything that we do to improve our own communities will impact that piece of the world in a positive way.

SUMMARY

It would be a much sadder world if no one knew how to share or had the impulse to give, especially if those who are gifted with a mind for technical innovation. We are all the benefactors of someone's inclination to transmit their genius into a product or service that makes our lives easier. Creativity, discovery and entrepreneurship should be encouraged and nurtured in the young and the old. The world is certainly a better place because of those who care enough to share their means, time and talents.

KEY IDEAS TO REMEMBER

- Every life is impacted by another.

- Some of our greatest technological advancements were the result of collaboration.

- Caring to share is the impetus of collaboration.

- A positive change in a single community counts as a change in a tiny piece of the world.

Part III:
The Consequences and Inspirations of Caring To Share
By
Steve Sonntag

Chapter 6 - For The Ones Being Helpers

In Latin, the infinitive "servare" means "to protect, store, keep, guard, preserve, serve, and watch over", as defined by www.latin-dictionary.net[2]. There are many people who are willing personally to be involved to make a significant difference for others so that their lives will be that much more fulfilling personally, academically, and professionally.

Many people have the primal instinct that "gets into gear" in order to do whatever it takes to make a difference for someone else. For instance, parents are very protective of their children. If parents see their unaware children about to encounter some kind of danger, they will immediately take action to prevent any injury or any tragedy from occurring.

Parents will also make a concerted effort to try to realistically fulfill their children's wishes, if and when there is enough money to afford their luxury items, such as their desired technological devices. If it is not possible, while children may feel disappointed, they will learn a valuable lesson, that life means sometimes having to wait a short time, a long time, or to make choices.

Parents may feel bad about delaying any wishes while some may rationalize this delay as a part of the human experience. They probably had similar experiences while they were growing up, although the times and the wishes were significantly different from nowadays.

Teachers are "in loco parentis" or 'in the place of a parent". They have a significant job to be acutely aware of their students in every respect along with doing their best to educate them. While the teachers' focus is primarily their students' education, the students' outside world can either offer a positive influence or a hindrance, thus possibly creating problems in the school environment.

This author has encountered many kinds of students and parents throughout the years. While most families have been very helpful with

---

2.   http://www.latin-dictionary.net

one another and for the sake of education, there have been significant numbers of students that have either sought the school environment as a safe haven or a place to take out their aggression. Recently, a former student sent me a lengthy message explaining how she had lived in a very dysfunctional family situation. Having not been given money for lunch, I gave her money so she could eat.

She continued to explain she was then pregnant. She now has several children, and she thanked me for caring enough and sharing as much as possible.

This previous example is one of a thousand examples that take place daily by teachers.

Acts of generosity have oftentimes been promoted even by presidents, such as by President John F. Kennedy, who said the following: "Ask not what your country can do for you, but what you can do for your country". President George H. W. Bush promoted the phrase of "a thousand points of light" to promote volunteerism, such as cleaning garbage alongside roads, highways, and freeways. Another way to help society on a local level is to volunteer in committees at local schools.

In the movie and the musical "Man of La Mancha", someone asks the squire of Don Quixote, Sancho Panza, why he is his sidekick when it seems as though he is not getting any compensation whatsoever. Sancho Panza responds with: "I like him." Such a question and such a response are indicative of what it means to be in a caring, sharing relationship. While it is good to gain something, relationships have always mattered and always will.

While there are many people who believe that "time is money" and that they should not do anything for nothing, there are many worthy causes that can be very helpful for different reasons. There may be personal reasons. There may be professional reasons. It may be that one truly does care that our world is a better place when we take the time and the energy to help one another. In turn, a form of "positive karma" may occur, although that may not be the ultimate reason for extending one's arms and one's heart to help others. One of the last chapters of this book deals with people and organizations that truly have cared and that truly have shared unselfishly.

This is not to say that we must completely avoid earning money, because that is being very unrealistic. We indeed do need money in order to survive and to thrive in this world. On the other hand, to go to the opposite extreme to say we should completely avoid donating our time, our energy, and yes even some of our money to help in need is living in isolation and can have dramatic consequences, whether they are small or enormous.

Moderation is very worthy of consideration. We can earn money so that we and our significant others will be provided for. We can also help others to help themselves by advising as needed, by encouraging, and by praising.

Such forms of generosity will bring smiles to the ones in need of help and to the helpers. When people take the initiative to do something out of the ordinary, an uncommon courtesy, whether it is something very small or something very big, the helpers can gain a sense of accomplishment. They feel that they have done something for the sake of humanity. In turn, the helpers will feel a little happier or quite a bit happier, especially when the ones who are being helped see the validity and the results of what the helpers are doing for others.

Indeed, this warmth of sunshine, this generosity to help someone else, truly can positively affect the helpers' lives.

As a consequence, such a validation of an accomplishment can easily result in more generous attempts for the sake of others when the time is right for other individuals. It is similar to a pendulum that once it hits pegs from one side, the consequences will be that the other pegs, in this case other people, can be slightly or dramatically affected in order to improve their lives and other people in their personal and quite possibly professional lives.

KEY IDEAS TO REMEMBER:

• Many people have the primal instinct that "gets into gear" in order to make a difference for someone else.

• There are many worthy causes.

• Generosity will bring smiles to the ones being helped and to the helpers.

Chapter 7 - What If They Don't Want To Be Helped?

There's an old saying: "You can lead a horse to water, but you can't make it drink it". You as the helper have the best of intentions to help someone else, although if the other person is not receptive to possibly changing, what can you do to change the mindset of the other person? Is it even possible?

To answer the above questions, one needs to evaluate the other person's situation, perspective, and attitude as much as you can. Their past may have been such that they can't readily accept the possibility that someone else can help them, although they appreciate the thought and the intent. Another possibility is that they may not necessarily trust anyone other than themselves. They may have been hurt so badly in one way or another, that they feel so dismayed or so depressed and not wanting anyone's help whatsoever.

Due to their past, they may have a negative attitude. They may perceive others as having malicious intentions and only wanting to deceive others for their own selfish reasons, even though the helper has the best of intentions. Even if the helper has a positive attitude, even the smallest fragment of doubt by the one needing help can easily cast doubt on the other person's best of intentions, thereby discounting all attempts to connect, to care, and to share.

If their current circumstance is such that they are in a dreadful relationship in which they feel helpless that is being very abusive and controlling, they may even feel scared due to any repercussions by the other person. They may feel so scared, feel so repressed, and/or feel so depressed, such as the Stockholm syndrome as was described in a previous chapter.

You as the willing giver are to be applauded for your ability to care by sharing what you have to offer. While you are applauded for your positive energy and your generosity, being sensitive to others and their situation will be very valuable in order to have a better understanding of another person.

If you perceive them as being ready to divulge their thoughts and their feelings, please take the opportunity to offer your help, although it needs to be done when and where you can talk with them privately, if at all possible.

It is then important to give them your full attention, to look at them, to give them their space while they are talking, to validate their feelings when it seems appropriate to do so, and any other caring approach that allows them to know that you are listening to them and to their feelings completely.

It is then your approach that needs to be considered. By you listening more, there is a better likelihood that they will be more revealing of their situation. In fact, they may share a lot that you don't necessarily know. By doing this, they will understand that you are the recipient of what they want you to know. They truly are venting their own frustrations about their lives, and that is what they critically need to do. They wish to resolve their situation, although they may feel helpless due to their circumstances.

Of course, it is important to be sensitive, to be patient, and not to inquire too much at first, because they may then tend to want to become withdrawn, the exact opposite of your purpose. By asking general questions, they may voluntarily share more of their innermost feelings.

If they are in a bad mood, this situation needs to be delicately assessed by you. In psychological terms, you need to have a good boundary, the ability "not to take it in" and realize what your intentions are. You are there for the sake of the people whom you recognize as needing help. People in a bad mood may want not to reveal anything about themselves at that moment, although if they are angry enough and/or frustrated enough, they may actually wish to divulge what is going on. It essentially needs then to be done in their own time, in their own way, and when they are ready to reveal their situation.

Think of them as volcanoes. If they are really "hot", they may explode. If so, it is best to keep your distance so that their anger does not flow in your direction, because you do not want their "hotness" or their anger to be taken out onto you. To continue with the analogy of volcanoes, if they are "smoldering", they may or may not want to reveal what is going on with them, although there is a lot beneath the surface that wants to appear, but not necessarily right now.

Here's another example. Think of yourself as a parent to an adult. Oftentimes, parents need to be patient and to guide as necessary. This is very much the same kind of philosophy as Kahlil Gibran who wrote *The Prophet* in which he states that parents are like bows that offer the guidance while the children are the arrows needing direction. People need to be willing to be placed in the right direction at the right time of their lives. How and when they intend to express whatever that is bothering them needs to be addressed with sensitivity, with patience, and with guidance when the time is right.

If you need to wait due to them not being in a good mood and not being open to any possible suggestions, from your perspective, this can be very hard to do. You wish them well and want to do the best for them as soon as possible.

If and when you take the initiative to divulge to them that you are very aware of something that is disturbing them but they are not receptive to reveal what is going on, you are at least having them be aware that you are aware of how they are. It is then when they need to make the decision, if and when they wish to discuss whatever is going on for them with you. On the other hand, this approach may backfire, because if you are too assertive without being sensitive, they may wish to "clam up" and to ask you to leave them alone.

If they reveal what is bothering them and if you are unable to help due to the severity of their situation, it is then suggested that you tactfully mention that they need to discuss their situation with a professional that can allow them to reveal their situation, if they do not have one already.

Being available to someone else speaks wonders about you. It shows that you care, although they probably know that already. While their initial reaction may be defensive and not to discuss their situation, they probably will respect you for being sensitive about them. It is only then hoped that they will come to the realization that they need to reach out to you and to accept your generous offer to be of assistance to them. Thank you when that happens! You truly can make a difference for them and quite possibly with them when they are receptive.

KEY IDEAS TO REMEMBER:

• You as the helper have the best intentions to help someone else.

• If the one needing help is reluctant to accept your help, you need to evaluate the other person's situation, perspective, and attitude as much as you can.

• People need to be willing to reveal whatever is bothering them.

• Being available to someone else speaks wonders about you.

Chapter 8 - The Benefits of Being Helped

Upon recognizing the need for help, receiving it, accepting it, and acting on the helper's suggestions, the benefits of being helped will blossom in so many ways. Following through on the helper's suggestions will vary based on the situation and the feelings of the person being helped.

On the other hand, even with the best of intentions, the one being helped may be reluctant to one degree or another in order to pursue doing something for their own good. This is somewhat similar to the movie *"Bless the Beasts and Children"* in which the ultimate objective of some children at a summer camp is to release some buffaloes from a fenced area; nevertheless, the buffaloes remain in the fenced area due to possibly feeling more comfortable there or knowing that they have food there. This again could be similar to the Stockholm situation.

These buffaloes are similar to people that are so accustomed to a certain way of living, that even though it is best to pursue something better, they may remain with the "tried and true", perhaps being afraid or very reluctant of something new to accept and to try, especially if there is a hostile significant other involved. For these reluctant individuals, it may take longer to encourage them to change. The operative word is "may", seeing that there are no guarantees, and it can be rather disappointing and frustrating for the person who cares and sees an inability of someone else to change due to however they perceive their circumstances.

When the person decides to pursue the suggestion after accepting the suggestion, this leads to many opportunities. They will have found a new purpose in their lives, and they deserve to be applauded for accepting and acting on advice for their own good.

On the other hand, they may go from being very unaware to being extremely aware, and they may actually focus so much so on their new purpose, that they may easily forget about the people that are a positive part of their lives. That is why it is very important to have them appreciate all of the positive people of their lives by continuing to devote quality time with them. Once moderation is attained so that their new purpose in their lives is balanced with the people that are important in their lives, there can be many benefits.

On a feeling level, they can have a better self-concept. There is a certain amount of joy and satisfaction for knowing that someone cared enough to inspire them for a new focus in life. Thus, they will feel positive instead of just living a day-by-day existence and with possible reluctance and/or with possible fear.

Having such a positive attitude allows people to realistically view life. They already acknowledge that there can be challenges in life, although there can be many challenges that can be overcome. People willing to make some sort of change can become empowered and thus fulfilled much more so, thus providing themselves more opportunities than anticipated.

With this new perspective about life, there is a new sense of purpose. People can become that much more organized in what they wish to accomplish. Under these circumstances, it is best to read, to internalize, and to use the book entitled *Write It Down: The Edge That Can Make You Stand Out* by German Gomez in which he explains very methodically and very practically how to achieve current goals and future goals.

By having a positive attitude, by being organized, and by having goals, this can result in being focused while allowing for creativity to be a part of life. In turn, by being flexible due to one's creativity, people can create the perfect plan and possibly the perfect result, although they need to take into account that there can be "stumbling blocks" along the way. That is why it is important to be flexible and receptive to anything that may transpire while focusing on the ultimate goal.

Permitting others to collaborate can result in that much more creativity and that much more acceptance of the plan. Such a collaborative effort can be very positive for everyone that is involved. It may mean being flexible and compromising, although it always needs to be remembered that everyone involved can have the same goal to achieve and to succeed.

What always needs to be remembered is what the past was like, who or what was inspirational, and to have an attitude of gratitude. Such a sensitivity of the past will allow people to remain humble in whatever is being pursued in the present time. These enlightened people need to express their gratitude directly to the people who cared enough to be aware of them and to make suggestions for change.

Also, it is suggested that while one is fulfilling one's dream or after succeeding in one's goals, to pay it forward to others so that they too can become inspired and to perfect their own abilities. This can be called the "positive snowball effect".

Awareness and willingness to care and to share will benefit someone else. You indeed can be the originator to help others so that they can help themselves as well as future generations . Thank you!

KEY IDEAS TO REMEMBER:

- The benefits of being helped will blossom in so many ways.

- They then can have a better self-concept.

- Having a positive attitude allows people to realistically view life.

- There is then a new sense of purpose.

- Collaboration can result in that much more creativity.

- Awareness and willingness to care and to share will benefit someone else.

Chapter 9 – The Personal Needs of Caring to Share

While caring and sharing with others are the ultimate goals for a better world, we too can be our own best care providers, because we know ourselves much better. We know our limitations. We know our "breaking points". We can extend ourselves out of our comfort zones. This can be noticed with people who "take the plunge" and do zip lining or to go on a daring amusement ride, for example.

At the same time that life is to be enjoyed and to be fulfilled, there can be times in which we need to slow down. People can and do become sick when they do too much. If you think of people that focus so much time and so much energy into their work and then take a vacation, it is possible to have a "melt down", exhaustion, or getting a cold. If so, people will be forced to stay in their homes for any amount of time or to quit their jobs completely.

While the above situation is extreme, this author attended a teacher conference once in which a school psychologist said that when people become physically ill by having a cold or the flu for example, they will usually stay home in order to recover. The school psychologist also recommended that if and when people are simply exhausted due to any personal or professional reasons so that it makes it a challenge to focus and to accomplish one's goals, that it is best to take time off from work in order to take care of oneself by simply relaxing all day or perhaps several days by using their sick days, if available.

Granted, this is easier said than done. While you are enthusiastic about something and are motivated to achieve, it is also extremely important to take care of yourself which also includes your physical health.

Moderation in terms of how you care and share is exceptionally important for yourself and for others around you. It is then that you will be able to care to the best of your ability along with being able to share as much as you can.

When one is healthy enough on a regular basis, knowledge is good, if we apply what we have learned for the purpose of helping others help themselves. Of course, the personal benefit of acquiring knowledge can be that of earning notoriety, wealth, and the possibility of further positive rewards.

When you are able to have collected all of this knowledge in one or more fields and when you are able to say the following: "How can I help you?", those five words in this simple question mean so very much.

First, the word "how" is powerful. What is implied is that you know the logic of the material so that you can begin in an easy way and to progress to the more complicated material in the best ways possible.

The second word "can" refers to your ability to help. In Spanish, "poder" means "to be able to, can". Also, in Spanish, "el poder" means "the power". Thus, you have the power within you to be of service to someone else, and your expertise can be to their benefit.

The third word "I" shows the other person that you of all people whom they know are making a concerted effort to take the time and the energy to do something for someone else.

The fourth word "help" is magical, because you can provide any number of resources that are available. Think of the word "help" as an acronym, meaning harmony, entitling, longing, planning". Harmony, because you and the other person are in sync to work together so that the other person will benefit. Entitling so that the other person can "take the ball and run with it". Longing, because you are willing to help someone else in order to improve in one way or another. Planning, meaning that you are guiding them in a methodical way so they can ultimately become self-actualizing and self-reliant.

The fifth and final word is "you", the precious person in need of assistance. You as the willing helper are there for as long as possible in order to help someone else catch and fulfill his or her dreams.

Such a very important question is open-ended, thus allowing the other person to know that it is now the best time to make some sort of change that will help their lives.

Combining these words with sincerity in the way the words are spoken with eye contact and with body language will show the intended receiver, the one needing help, that there is an important connection between the two of you and that there is an opportunity "to run with it" and to gain from caring and sharing.

Family can truly be a very valuable resource for you when you perceive each other as being able to care and being able to share. After all, they are your first known people on this planet who have seen you through your good and possibly your not-so-good times.

In order to maximize the family environment that much more so as a place of love, comfort, and fun, it is suggested to consider the following activity on a monthly basis as much as possible.

One family member, the youngest first to the oldest last, develops a half-day or a full day of activities for the entire family as a complete surprise. It can be an activity with no cost, little cost, or a maximum amount to be spent for the entire family. Money management, where things are, time management, making sure there's enough gas in the vehicle, and weather need to be considered.

Since the family is vital for the preservation of the current and future societies, here are several books that can benefit the family environment and can also be a lot of fun for parties and trips. The first book is *The Kids' Book of Questions* by Gregory Stock. It deals with many hypothetical questions to which there are no correct answers. These questions are designed to give situations that happen in children's lives that can present challenges. It is then that they need to make decisions as to what to do or not to do.

Here is an example of a question from that book. This author has given workshops to schools. One time at an elementary school, there was an after school meeting that included some 60 students, parents, administrators, and teachers. I asked for one child to volunteer to select a question, and the parent was with the child. One child selected the following question from this book: "If you were the principal of this school, what change would you make?" The 4th or 5th grade girl responded with "more homework" while her father responded with "more playtime". Indeed, one never knows what a person is thinking or feeling until they are asked.

The second book, *The Book of Questions* also by Gregory Stock, consists of more adult issues, and such a book may be useful for more mature teens that can see "the big picture" when it comes to society and adult issues as well as for adults.

The reason for suggesting these two books is that when we are presented with challenges, these situations show that no matter how indifferent people may appear to be, they do react, thus caring to one degree or another. When there are situations that are presented and when people make conclusions, this is the moment in which some sort of decision can be made.

Friends by their very definition can be very helpful for you, if and when you need help. They are there for you during your good times and during the times that you need someone to allow you to vent and to get guidance for whatever troubles you or for whatever you need insight. While caring is very beneficial and while sharing can be the final outcome by the helper, providing comfort by just listening can be very helpful as well. Perhaps by doing so, the one needing help can solve the problem.

Society regards going to the doctor for physical care in order to resolve any health issue, and that is extremely important to do. To disregard one's physical being is harmful and detrimental to oneself and quite possibly shorten one's life. So, when you do have any health issue, no matter what anyone else may say or try to persuade you to do, you need to be your best advocate and to be assertive to seek the help from your primary doctor at first.

We all have the primal instinct to survive in the best ways possible. For the most part of our lives, we can do very well even with the "bumps in the road", the times in which there are issues and tragedies. If and when there is a need to be comforted and if and when family members and friends are unable to provide the support you need, it is best to seek a counselor in order to discuss and to eventually resolve any or all challenges. It is important to realize resolution takes time and patience for oneself and for others.

Generally speaking, society regards getting traditional forms of counseling as a so-called weakness, although it is vital and comforting. When there are physical issues, we seek the help from doctors. When there are emotional issues, it is important to seek guidance from professionals.

Another suggestion to consider is both physically and emotionally helpful, although it can be rather exhausting as well. It is called Myofascial Release Therapy (MFR) at www.myofascialrelease.com[3]. There can be one or two professionals that allow you to either lie down on a table or to sit on the table in order for you to talk about anything you wish, whether it is personal or professional. It is a safe, confidential environment where you are accepted for who you are.

When involving yourself in this process, you may become so much in touch with your feelings, thereby releasing or cleansing them so that there are no distractions for your creativity and for your goals in life. In fact, by you just expressing yourself, you may be able to resolve any issues, or, if you are so inclined, you may want to ask for suggestions. It does require a person wishing to be totally open with one's feelings, and that may be rather challenging, at least at first. Yet, it can be done when so inclined, especially after establishing a rapport with the professionals.

Child Protective Services provides a way to protect the young who need advocates and shelters when needed. After all, the mental,

---

3.   http://www.myofascialrelease.com

emotional, physical, and sexual wellbeing of the young will mean that they will have a better life now and in the future for themselves as well as for others whom they encounter and whom they cherish.

While the young deserve to be cared for, it is just as important adults and senior citizens to be cared for. An unfortunate reality is that there is elder abuse, and there are luckily many county agencies that protect elders. It is extremely important for family and friends knowing of elders being abused to call any county agency that protects as soon as possible.

Everyone deserves to be cared for authentically and always
KEY IDEAS TO REMEMBER:

- We can be our own best care providers.

- There can be times in which we need to slow down.

- Moderation in terms of how you care and share is exceptionally important for yourself and for others around you.

- Knowledge is good, when we apply what we have learned for the purpose of helping others help themselves.

- "How can I help you?" means so very much by being an open invitation for others to know someone else cares.

- Family and friends can be vital resources.

- Taking care of one's physical health is essential.

- Counseling of one form or another is essential.

- Everyone deserves to be cared fo authentically and always.

Chapter 10 – The Global Needs of Caring to Share

There are many resources on a global scale that are very valuable for the sake of groups of people along with some very caring and sharing individuals for the sake of humankind. What is very noteworthy is the abundance of goodness that does exist.

The United Nations has many important parts in order to help humankind. One of them is UNICEF at www.unicefusa.org which allows for support for children in underdeveloped countries.

Educational organizations, such as the Future Teachers of America at www.futureteachers.org[4], the National Education at www.nea.org[5], and the American Federation of Teachers at www.aft.org[6] are concerned about teaching and learning trends so that current generations of students will benefit from their teachers' instruction and will thus become inspired to become productive citizens in our global society in their adult lives.

Even when teachers become established and organized enough to feel they don't necessarily wish to be helped, there are so many more resources that are available for their consideration. There are textbook companies that have teacher resource materials, websites, and apps to complement the teaching and the learning of new material.

There are current teachers and mentors in school districts that have a wealth of information and a wealth of expertise. Many teachers oftentimes will be receptive to new ways of teaching and learning. On the other hand, there are teachers who are set in their ways, and it is only hoped that they will consider and use at least some, if not all, of the ideas, websites, and apps that are available to improve student learning. Current teachers and retired teachers have been speakers in classes, all of which can make students realize that there are many adults that are aware of and are inspired by the information being shared.

---

4.   http://www.futureteachers.org

5.   http://www.nea.org

6.   http://www.aft.org

For those teachers who are retired, there can be many opportunities for them to give individual attention to both teachers and students. With the administration's approval, retired teachers can become mentors to new teachers, "guides on the side" as Dr. Roger Taylor proclaimed. With the administration's approval, retired teachers can tutor students that struggle with the concepts of classes. Tutors can also help with different subjects at the local libraries.

Current teachers and retired teachers have another great option, and that is to tutor with WyzAnt at www.wyzant.com[7], which is a great resource for people of all ages to become more knowledgeable about different subjects both in person and online.

Another noteworthy group is Teachers Without Borders at www.teacherswithoutborders.org. This group includes initiatives, free courses, and internships.

Curriki at www.curriki.org[8] is the free exchange of ideas by teachers throughout the world. Teachers Pay Teachers at www.teacherspayteachers.com[9] provides the exchange of ideas for teachers whereby teachers can post ideas, and whenever other teachers wish to use these ideas, they pay a nominal fee to download them. In turn, the teachers with the ideas earn extra money which is always nice!

The National Parent Teacher Association at www.pta.org[10] is also deserving of praise as an advocate for the entire educational community with their local school groups, with their state conventions, and with their national conventions, all for the support of parents, for the sake of the children who will be our society's adults, and for the sake of the school.

There are many high schools that require students to complete so many hours of community service in one form or another on a yearly

---

7.   http://www.wyzant.com

8.   http://www.curriki.org

9.   http://www.teacherspayteachers.com

10.   http://www.pta.org

basis. While this may be viewed by students as another assignment to fulfill amongst their demanding, academic load of classes, they do understand the importance of giving back to the community to those who are not as fortunate as they are. There have been many instances in which these students have become so inspired by these forms of caring to share, that they actually become professionals of those organizations.

An unfortunate reality for youth is bullying both in school as well as outside school. Fortunately, schools have preventative measures in place in order to deal with such challenges, such as peer resource groups. Also, with the help of the Internet, I Can Help at www.icanhelpdeletenegativity.org[11] is a great way to help students confronting cyberbullying and anything else that can be harmful for students.

In the realm of education, accreditation, which is the evaluation of the entire school community, needs to be earned every 6 years. There is a lot of time and a lot of energy that are expended by the school personnel, students, and parents into developing a report indicating all positive segments of the school community and determining what improvements are needed. The school going through the accreditation process is expected to fulfill all of the necessary work in a timely fashion.

An accreditation team of administrators, teachers, sometimes parents, and sometimes students usually will not know each other. They will receive the school's report. They independently study it and subsequently write their preliminary findings.

The actual visitation by the accreditation team takes place over a 3½ day period of time, which includes meeting with different groups of the school community. They ask for comments. They ask questions. They jot down notes, although like judges, they do not reveal their final decision.

---

11.   http://www.icanhelpdeletenegativity.org

The accreditation team also does its best to observe all classes throughout their visit in order to understand how teachers interact with their students along with how well the students are engaged in the learning process. It has also been encouraged for the accreditation team observers to write a brief note upon viewing each class and to lay the note on the teacher's desk. In this way, they are being validated for what they are doing, which is a lot, when you consider teachers design lesson plans, deal with classroom management, paperwork, evaluations, and meetings.

It is only when the accreditation team meets each afternoon and each evening, that they confer in order to evaluate their findings. It is only after the gathering as much information as possible, that they meet privately at the school typically in a conference room and at their hotel where they stay in order to determine independently how well the school is functioning overall.

At the end of this 3½ day visit, they relate the school's strengths and areas of concern as had been determined by the school with any other findings to the school community, although they do not disclose the term or the amount of time for the school's accreditation. The main accreditation office reads and determines, if they wish to agree with the findings of the accreditation team, and the main accreditation office determines the length of the school's accreditation. In turn, the main accreditation office informs the school of the length of their accreditation.

Once the school is deemed to be accredited or validated based on all of the findings, the students' classes and diplomas are considered worthy and fully accepted for their work at the school site. Then, the school has its own areas of improvement for which they decide how to resolve what they and the accreditation team have determined to be valid and necessary for the sake of the entire school community.

The accreditation team's transportation, lodging, and meals are taken care of completely by the school itself.

Before taking time off from their normal responsibilities, they probably have some additional work to do for their regular work, if they work. People could logically say that since the accreditation team is not being compensated for their time, their work reading the school's report, and developing their own evaluation, above and beyond their basic expenses being completely paid for, that it is an incredible waste of time for the team.

While the work can be enormous and time consuming, the accreditation team members can say that they are benefiting from the experience as well. It is almost like a working vacation. The team oftentimes is able to discuss common concerns by meeting people whom they haven't known previously. They may wish to communicate with them in the future. They may even wish to bring newly learned ideas to their own school campus. People can know that their work is being appreciated. Overall, it is a very mutually beneficial experience.

Bill and Melinda Gates have earned enormous amounts of money that they could have simply spent on themselves. While there are tax advantages for their generosity, they have developed special scholarships for 300 minority high school seniors. They must feel a great deal of satisfaction in order to be able to give back to the community, knowing that the recipients will have the opportunity of becoming more educated, to prosper in their adult years, and thus to become significant members for their future society. For more information about this scholarship, please go to www.thegatesscholarship.org[12].

There are so many other scholarships that are offered for one's consideration that are generously offered and given, and it is best to do a Google search for those scholarships that are the most appropriate for your consideration. If you have high school age children, it is best to have them check online, to listen to the daily bulletin, and to go to the counselor's office for possible scholarships that are available and

---

12.   http://www.thegatesscholarship.org

to determine when the applications are due. Also, it is exceptionally important to adhere to all of the requirements in order to be considered.

Some local and national organizations, such as the Red Cross at www.redcross.org[13] and United Way at www.unitedway.org[14], are very generous with their time and with their money so that others will have better opportunities without ever wanting to be compensated or expecting anything in return. When there are natural phenomena happening, such as hurricanes, floods, fires, and earthquakes, there are oftentimes organizations that will start collecting donations that will help the innocent victims.

In terms of the hospital setting, there are oftentimes volunteers who are retired individuals that will direct visitors and incoming patients to wherever they need to go. There are also volunteers who will go to the patients' rooms in order to deliver newspapers and drinks. Such volunteers are oftentimes not paid for their services, although they provide guidance and comfort for the ones in need. These volunteers are making a difference with everyone needing to be in the hospital.

There are many children's hospitals that offer surgeries for the young for little or no cost. For example, St. Jude's Hospital at www.stjude.org[15] is a wonderful hospital that provides care and comfort for children and for their parents while supplying surgeries. Another great example of a compassionate, caring hospital is the Shriners Hospital that will accept children with medical issues, regardless of the families' ability to pay. For more details, please go to www.shrinershospitalsforchildren.org/shc[16].

---

13.   http://www.redcross.org

14.   http://www.unitedway.org

15.   http://www.stjude.org

16.   http://www.shrinershospitalsforchildren.org/shc

Related to how people can work together when it comes to health matters, Hayden Hatfield Ryals became a national marrow donor. She became a bone marrow match for a 3 year old girl by the name of Skye. Hayden then asked her and her parents, if Skye could be the flower girl at Hayden's wedding, and this was the case. Such a very generous gift by a bride to a girl whom she had never met is truly a caring to share gift. If you are interested in being a marrow donor, please go to www.bethematch.org[17].

Another fabulous organization for children who are diagnosed with a critical illness is Make-A-Wish. They state: "In the United States and its territories, on the average, a wish is granted every 34 minutes." Due to people who donate, volunteers, and supporters, they have been able to make children's wishes realized. Such caring and sharing truly are extremely commendable. For more information, please go to www.wish.org[18].

The Ronald McDonald House at www.rmhc.org[19] provides a fabulous support system for those families wishing to be close to their very ill children that need to be in the hospital, spending several weeks to several months. Such a house allows families to provide comfort to their very ill children that need to remain hospitalized, and the families feel very appreciative of this sensitivity and such kindness offered.

A wonderful organization is Doctors Without Borders at www.doctorswithoutborders.org[20]. It is an international, humanitarian, medical, non-governmental organization that consists of medical personnel that will work outside the city limits in order to help people that live there and that cannot afford becoming healthier. It is due to their generosity, that they are very much praised for their generous dedication.

---

17.   http://www.bethematch.org

18.   http://www.wish.org

19.   http://www.rmhc.org

20.   http://www.doctorswithoutborders.org

Another very kind way that people donate their time and their energy is by helping children and adults the activities of the Special Olympics. Races and an assortment of activities related to the Special Olympics are heartwarming for all concerned. If you are interested, please go to www.specialolympics.org[21].

Easter Seals at www.easterseals.com[22] is an outstanding organization that helps those individuals who have some sort of physical condition in which they need to improve their physical wellbeing.

Docents at museums oftentimes are unpaid. They simply enjoy explaining the different exhibits to the visitors that are available, because they are very knowledgeable of what others are viewing. In turn, these docents provide that much more of an appreciation to what the visitors are viewing. Again, this is a very mutually beneficial experience.

People oftentimes will donate to specific causes due to the goodness of their hearts or due to personal reasons. Charity walks and runs provide many benefits. First, such walks and runs are organized for specific causes, such as for diabetes, cancer, and Alzheimer's research. Secondly, the participants advertise these events to people in order to gain funds based on how many miles they go, for example. Thirdly, the people contributing to such causes become happy to donate to such worthy causes. Lastly, the participants are happy due to being able to help with such worthy causes along with the benefit of exercising and meeting others in the process.

In order to help individuals and causes, while one could consider getting loans from people and banks, a very good way to connect on the Internet is with the help of Go Fund Me at www.gofundme.com[23]. This is a way to start fundraising almost instantly.

21.	http://www.specialolympics.org

22.	http://www.easterseals.com

23.	http://www.gofundme.com

Another such fabulous Internet website is Global Giving at www.globalgiving.org[24] which connects donors with projects throughout the world.

Volunteering at soup kitchens oftentimes at churches is very beneficial for all concerned. The people who rely on such meals are very grateful for the food that is being provided. The organizers and the servers at soup kitchens know their work is contributing to the good health of people in need. If you are interested in this kind of activity, it is best to check with your local community's website for more details.

Donating your time at a homeless shelter where there are typically destitute individuals and families is an eye opening experience. Just listening to these individuals and families can be very helpful for them, because they oftentimes feel hopeless and helpless. Perhaps, you may be able to provide them with suggestions, although it is best not to become personally or financially involved. Again, it is best to check with your local community's website for more details.

Women's centers oftentimes house those individuals who had been in abusive relationships. They live in these shelters in order to regain their self-respect and to restore their self-confidence. They will oftentimes have speakers that can be very inspirational and very helpful so that these women will be able to become fully independent. For more details, it is best to check with your county's website.

While women unfortunately are victimized, men also have been abused. It may seem to consider this possibility; however, there have been instances in which men become overpowered by women who may sense and feel superior than their partners. Such manipulation, whether it is done slowly or over time, can make men feel inferior. That is why there are men's shelters available in order to comfort and to regain their self-respect and to restore their self-confidence. For more details, it is best to check with the county's website.

---

24.   http://www.globalgiving.org

No matter what gender, sexual orientation, color, or nationality a person may be, everyone deserves to be treated humanely and fairly. For any unfortunate victims, it will take one abusive situation that is "so over the top", that the person will say "enough is enough" and move away from the situation. It is being courageous; nevertheless, as many a counselor will say, you need to take care of yourself and to be self-full. It is preserving your physical well-being and your sanity. There are people who definitely care and will definitely share to the best of their ability so that they will become more self-assured in order to have a more fulfilling life.

Since there are many single parents, there is a great website for them and their children. It is called Big Brothers Big Sisters at www.bbbs.org[25]. Adults that are determined safe by the government are connected with single parents and their children. This big brother or big sister meets with the single parent and child in order to be interviewed. If everyone is in agreement, this big brother or big sister meets with the child on a regular basis so that the child is able to express how he or she feels and what his or her daily life is like. The importance of these regular meetings is so that the child is able to know that someone cares by listening to them.

Related to mentoring in our society, www.mentoring.org[26] is a great way to contribute your skills to others in need. Such an ability to care and thus to share with others can be the exact inspiration and revitalization of others so that they can become fully engaged in society.

Veteran service organizations are wonderful due to their compassion and due to their care for those who serve their country for the greater good and for the protection of their people.

There are famous people in society, including movie stars and sports team players, that have contributed to those in need or simply

---

25.   http://www.bbbs.org

26.   http://www.mentoring.org

have health issues. For example, they have gone to hospitals and worldwide tragedies to provide comfort to the young patients there.

There are many very inspiring individuals who have made a positive impact in our society and deserve to be revered for their caring and sharing ways.

Fred Rogers, typically known as Mr. Rogers, was an extremely important, stable figure on television for many children throughout the years. His simple ways of presenting the complexities of life made it so very easy for the young to have a better appreciation of everyone and everything. For more information about him, please go to www.pbskids.org/rogers[27].

Another great way to touch the hearts of children in order to accept the beauty around them is the fabulous Sesame Street that has given many recognizable characters, such as Big Bird, Bert, Ernie, Oscar the Grouch, and Grover. The very fact that they have been producing these shows since 1969 speaks volumes to its importance. For more information, please go to www.pbskids.org/sesame[28].

Oprah Winfrey is truly a very inspirational person who cares by sharing, with her network, her O magazine, and her films, for example. For more information about her, please go to www.oprah.com[29].

Although he regrettably has passed, Wayne Dyer's philosophy was that of living up to your potential. He truly was a very motivational speaker and writer. For more details about him, please go to www.drwaynedyer.com[30].

Jack Canfield and Mark Hansen have been outstanding in their efforts to share the ideas of all kinds of people and professionals, and they have been able to help validate people's worth. For more information about their books, please go to www.chickensoup.com[31].

27.　　http://www.pbskids.org/rogers

28.　　http://www.pbskids.org/sesame

29.　　http://www.oprah.com

30.　　http://www.drwaynedyer.com

Dr. Louise Hay has been a very inspirational author and the founder of Hay House that has been producing many self-help books that show people do care by sharing their ideas. Being as selective as they are, her book company is continuing fabulously well. For more information about her and possibly to become a published writer through Hay House, please go to www.louisehay.com[32].

Related to physical issues that can be challenging, there are two very inspirational people that had very bad accidents, but were able to overcome them very well.

The first person is very well known by the name of Christopher Reeve and was thrown by his horse, thus paralyzing him. After having his surgery, it was his attitude that inspired him and thus was able to inspire others. His book *Nothing Is Impossible* is very worthwhile for you to read, because you will be inspired due to the fact that he didn't allow his injury to define him. He defined himself by his positive attitude, by what he did for others, and by what he had to offer to others.

The second person is not very well known, and his name is Grant Korgan. He had suffered a very bad skiing accident. He also had surgery and a lot of time devoted to physical therapy. He got a tremendous amount of support from family and friends, and he was ultimately able to improve himself quite a bit. In fact, he developed a workshop about overcoming obstacles and being better than one's circumstances.

Grant Korgan wrote a very realistic, very inspirational book called *Two Feet Back,* dealing with the fact that had he landed two feet back from where he landed, he would have been safe. It was his own great, personal stamina that helped to improve, although it was not always an easy path. It took a lot of time and a lot of effort to become better than his circumstances. He thus has been able to help others feel better.

---

31.   http://www.chickensoup.com

32.   http://www.louisehay.com

Of course, there are numerous generous individuals that have taken the initiative to leave whatever profession they have practiced and have donated a lot of their time, a lot of their energy, and a lot of their money to specific groups. To give you an example of the goodness of people that do care and take it to the next step by sharing, please go to www.cnn.com[33] to the heroes that have truly helped many different causes.

The Salvation Army at www.salvationarmyusa.org[34] and Goodwill Industries International, Inc. at www.goodwill.org[35] provide great services to those individuals that wish to improve their lives in different ways, no matter what their circumstances may have been or what they may be currently.

The National Association for the Advancement of Colored People at www.naacp.org[36] is a fantastic organization to help African Americans to protect them by having equal rights and eliminating racial hatred and racial discrimination.

The American Civil Liberties Union at www.aclu.org[37] is another fantastic organization to help everyone by defending and preserving the individual rights and liberties of everyone.

The Southern Poverty Law Center. www.splcenter.org[38] is a very powerful, very compassionate organization that serves those who have had the unfortunate experiences of dealing with any sort of discrimination.

Alcoholic Anonymous at www.aa.org[39] is another excellent organization to help those individuals with alcohol issues who want

---

33.   http://www.cnn.com

34.   http://www.salvationarmyusa.org

35.   http://www.goodwill.org

36.   http://www.naacp.org

37.   http://www.aclu.org

38.   http://www.splcenter.org

39.   http://www.aa.org

to improve their lives without having to rely on alcohol. While people have the best of intentions not to be tempted to drink, there are times in which they will resort to drinking again. Alcoholic Anonymous is a compassionate group of people that understands the ups and downs of life and are willing to help in the best possible, healthy ways of living without drinking.

Along with alcohol, other drug addiction issues such as legal and illegal substances have become rampant in our society due to any number of reasons. That is why many local groups have been developed to help these addicted individuals that want to help themselves.

Associated with alcohol and substance addiction, there are many organizations that support family members and friends who are directly and indirectly affected by these drug abusers.

The Innocence Project at www.innocenceproject.org[40] helps those individuals who feel they were wrongly convicted of crimes so that they can possibly be released from jail.

Adult Protective Services provides a way to protect the elderly from any kind of abuse imposed by relatives and friends.

As a way to improve one's life and also to help others help themselves, there is a terrific website called the Loving Healing Press Books at www.lovinghealing.com[41]. You can either write for their journal called "Recovering The Self", or there may be a possibility to write books for them, based on if and when they may wish to be open to that possibility. Even if you decide not to write for them, they have many articles and books for your consideration in order to love oneself and in order to heal oneself.

Hospice at www.hospicefoundation.org[42] is another outstanding organization that provides comfort and support for terminally ill individuals and for their families. Hospice oftentimes will even be able

---

40.   http://www.innocenceproject.org

41.   http://www.lovinghealing.com

42.   http://www.hospicefoundation.org

to work with local pharmacies to bring medications to the homes where the terminally ill individuals reside with no costs whatsoever.

The Compassionate Friends at www.compassionatefriends.org[43] is a great organization that helps families and friends deal with the unfortunate demise of their loved ones. They have local chapters, state conferences, national conferences, and international conferences that are all guided typically by counselors who have also lost loved ones.

Ask Me Anything at www.amafeed.com[44] is a great resource for people in order to share their questions and their concerns. In turn, knowledgeable people throughout the world can provide their perspectives.

TED at www.ted.com[45] are "conferences that post talks online for free distribution, under the slogan 'ideas worth spreading.'" This is an ideal platform in order to share ideas that can help people from a personal level to a global scale.

Help A Reporter at www.helpareporter.com[46] is a great website in which reporters are always looking for caring people who are knowledgeable in biotechnology, health care, entertainment, media, high technology, education, lifestyle, fitness, public policy, and government. If selected, they are interviewed for possible publication in magazine articles and books.

Another way to share your ideas for the sake of others is by checking with your local newspaper reporters in order to see if they are amenable to what you wish to share.

Related to magazine articles and books, being able to care and thus to share your ideas can help people help themselves. While it does take time to organize and to write your ideas for the sake of humanity, such a worthy endeavor is a great way to give back and to

---

43.   http://www.compassionatefriends.org

44.   http://www.amafeed.com

45.   http://www.ted.com

46.   http://www.helpareporter.com

inspire others. For more details on the process and the different ways to publish, it is best to go to the Writer's Market website for more details at www.writersmarket.com[47].

If you are more of a verbal person rather than a writer and if you wish to share your ideas, you may wish to consider being a speaker on the media, such as on You Tube at www.youtube.com[48], iHeartRadio at www.iheart.com[49], and the National Public Radio at www.npr.org[50], all of which include fountains of possibilities in order to relate information and to inspire people for a better, more informed life.

In our global society, we have had many caring and sharing individuals who have gained their fame due to their genuine humanity. Outside the United States, such people as Oskar Schindler, Mahatma Gandhi, Mother Teresa, and Malala Yousafzai have shown their ability to be authentic, inspirational, and helpful. Within the United States, Rosa Parks and Martin Luther King Jr. also demonstrated by their actions that they were totally focused on serving their society by their words and by their actions. Needless to say, there are thousands of humanitarians in the world whose focus is to help others help themselves.

The United Nations is a vital organization that can be very useful to help others and to seek justice, if and when there is a need. Granted, they are also immersed in politics that can impede their desire to help, although these individuals in the United Nations do their best to be the humane helpers of the world and wish to have equality and fairness for everybody. That is why such a global organization still exists, even though it has its struggles due to conflicts throughout the world.

A very unique website that helps people learn and to give back to the global society is Free Rice at www.freerice.com[51]. For every correct

---

47.   http://www.writersmarket.com

48.   http://www.youtube.com

49.   http://www.iheart.com

50.   http://www.npr.org

answer that is chosen, 10 grains of rice are raised to help end world hunger through the World Food Programme. You are encouraged to participate in this website due to it being a lot of fun, very educational, and very helpful.

While people of all ages deserve the appropriate care and attention, animals deserve the same appropriate care and attention. An outstanding organization, such as the Society for the Prevention of Cruelty to Animals, at www.spcai.org[52], allows caring people to share their humanity to animals while they wait for homes and in order to find homes where they can be cared for and loved.

Many animals have been trained to be sensitive to their masters in terms of illnesses. Many animals have been allowed to be comforting both at airports and on planes for those individuals that become nervous about flying. Many animals have been used in hospitals to be comforting for the patients. their family members, and their friends.

Above and beyond these specialty dogs, while pets can be a lot of work, they also have a great way of being trusted companions. For example, when and if you have had a rather stressful day, you can go home to your pet that only wants to be fed, to be loved, and to be cared for.

It is by being unconditional, by being humane, by being generous, and by being authentic that we can help each other, all of which is very inspirational and thus promotes goodwill amongst everyone. All of these programs and individuals are just a mere sample of the enormous wealth of kindness and generosity that does exist in our world.

KEY IDEAS TO REMEMBER:

---

51.   http://www.freerice.com

52.   http://www.spcai.org

• There are many people, books, organizations, and websites that are beneficial for improving the human condition.

• Pets have a great way of being trusted companions, whether we are in a good mood or in a not so good mood.

• It is by being unconditional, by being humane, by being generous, and by being authentic that we can help each other, all of which is very inspirational and thus promotes goodwill amongst everyone.

Chapter 11 - Personal Shares About Caring to Share

A variety of people were asked to ponder some questions about caring and sharing in their lives. This chapter is devoted to these questions and their personal shares or responses. We truly appreciate their time to respond and their insights for your sake.

Tara - Parent and Self-employed

1) How has your past influenced you to do what you are doing or what you have done?

2) Is there anyone in the past and/or currently who has influenced you to be the sharing, caring kind of person who you are?

Answers for both #1 and #2: "Blessed is he who preferreth his brother before himself." – Abdu'l-Baha (Baha i Writings)

The Golden Rule is universal among all the great Teachers (Manifestations) of God. Indeed, we were created to love one another and strive every day to do better than the day before. I feel blessed to have been raised in a home and community where our virtues and character were more important than our grades. My parents, grandparents and the Baha I Faith played an integral part in giving me the firm foundation of character I try to improve on and instill in my own children.

3. How have you been able to show that you care to share?

Although far from perfect, I have seen the effect a simple act of kindness has on both the recipient and myself. Whether the act is just a friendly smile and uplifting comment to a stranger or going out of my way to do something "big" for someone, I know it makes my dare more joyful and hopefully does the same for the person.

4. What have been the consequences of your ability to share? Will that experience influence your future decisions to share?

Consequences of desire to share have been the blessing of true friends who are themselves people that care to share. Friendships that have only strengthened over time and ones that are sincere and selfless. The desire to share is really not a conscious step, but one that at this point in life is just a part of who I am. So, yes, it will naturally influence future decisions.

5. How have you been able to give to others while not overdoing it?

The most precious gift to give, in my opinion, is future generations that are also natural lovers of humanity. I feel blessed that my children are also ones who hold the door for a stranger, remember to say thank you with a smile often prefer their sibling or friend over themselves. Not sure about overdoing – the world needs more love and unity!

6. What advice would you give to others who will be reading this book so that they have a more fulfilling life of giving and caring for themselves and for others?

Make every day richer (better) than the day before. Don't get on yourself, if you didn't do well today. Just try a little harder.

Miklos- Education Specialist

1. How has your past influenced you to do what you are doing or what you have done?

I divide the past into three categories: people, events and choices. They are all connected by a definite through-line.

To be honest, I don't think about the past that much. If I did, I wouldn't be able to truly live to the fullest in the moment I am now in. I reflect on the past only insofar as much as it inspires me to make now as great as the past that has brought me to this point, for better or for worse.

People

My family has influenced me by being a model, both for positive and negative things. There are parts of my parents that I always knew I wanted to be, and there were parts I knew I never wanted to be. That has influenced me by making me stop and reflect on my actions, sometimes even as I am engaging in them.

My teachers have influenced me in much the same way, except I had less emotional connection to them because they were "other" grown-ups that were not part of my family. For that reason, I tended to take their guidance more objectively. I could look at them as a model and either want to emulate them or not based mostly on objective observation. I rarely got emotional about a teacher the way I would about my parents, and I think that may just be because of family connection.

The influence, therefore, was all in me. For example, on a Saturday afternoon in the autumn of 1990 the phone rang at my family's house while I was outside mowing the lawn. I was a sophomore in high school and my drama teacher was calling to ask if I'd be interested in running the light board for the community theater play she directed. I was, so I took her offer. Little did I know that accepting that offer would set off a chain of events in my life.

My teacher didn't directly influence me per se. I accepted a challenge, an invitation to try something I had never considered. Later I would learn that accepting those invitations is what many people call taking opportunities.

The people in my life have influenced me by showing me opportunities. My parents and teachers showed me what can happen when you choose to accept or decline those opportunities. My friends and acquaintances advised me on what potential outcomes could be. The past experiences that were created by saying yes to every possible opportunity have become the greatest influence; namely, the education gained through living life.

Events

The events that influence and shape your life are out of your control. What you do in the face of joyous or tragic events both shape you and define you because you cannot practice for how you will react to the most important events of your life.

Events have influenced me by revealing my character to me. Sometimes it was reaffirming, other times it was humiliating. Still other times it was confusing, depressing, beguiling and exciting all at the same time.

For example, when I was 29, a good friend, who was just a few years older than me, died suddenly from a brain aneurism. I was out on a Saturday night with my girlfriend having a great time when I got a phone call from my friend's employee saying he didn't show up to the restaurant so she went to his house and found him on the floor. She called the last number on his cell phone, which was me.

The next thing I knew I was at the hospital with a doctor and others saying this would be the last time we saw him. The following night was a wake, then the funeral. It all happened within days.

Many people in my life have died, but that experience was influential because it made me realize how we can be enjoying life one moment and be dead the next. My father had passed away just prior to that, but the influence wasn't the same because he lived a long, full life and we were all ready to say goodbye.

When my friend died, I didn't make any big promises or proclamations. I just made a decision inside myself to live every day fully and remember to do good so that I never have regrets. That was 14 years ago.

Choices

I believe that what makes humans special, what makes our existence special, is that we have control over our own reactions. Whatever the world gives us, whether it is wealth, beauty, pain, death, joy or opportunity, what makes us human is the ability to do something with that.

My choices have influenced me by revealing that to be true; that we are able to choose how we live in the life we are given.

What I am doing now is a result of the inner influences of an immense web of my own choices and the outside influences of the people and events in my life.

I don't consider my life, family or work to be the result of influences in my life; rather, I consider it all to be the result of my reactions to all of those influences.

Had I reacted a different way anywhere along the way, today's life would be different.

However, since I don't usually think about the past, the what-ifs rarely if ever occur to me. The only thing that is of any value is now and what choices we make in it.

2. Is there anyone in the past and/or currently who has influenced you to be the sharing, caring kind of person who you are?

Too many to mention.

I want to note that the kind, caring people in my life have been as influential as the cruel ones.

Without the positive, caring teachers, friends, family, co-workers and others in my life I would not be the human being I am who is trying to find new paths to empathy and kindness each day.

However, it is also thanks to the people in my life who have brought torment and misery that I have been able to see into a world that is the opposite of the one I am working to create.

I think having a perspective where you can see as many sides of the world as possible is critical to being effective as an agent of positive change.

If I had to name just one person, I would say that my son is the biggest influence. He is both the result and the reason for everything having to do with sharing and caring. He would not exist if it weren't for the chances I took in caring. His future success in carrying on a legacy of empathy rests in the influences he gets from my wife and I, which come from the influences we received, and so on. It's all connected.

3. How have you been able to show that you care to share?

Smiling, hugging, listening and showing empathy.

I love smiling, and I often get feedback from people saying that my smiling made them feel good.

Hugging isn't something I used to be comfortable with, but I made a decision to change that. So, I am. I hug people whenever possible (and appropriate). It's a wonderful way to physically share your caring.

Listening is not a strength of mine. I love to speak and share ideas. Deep listening is a skill that must be practiced. When another person feels you are listening to them deeply, they know you care about them.

Showing empathy means all of the above and more. To me it means not just saying "I understand" to someone but doing something about it. My wife is pregnant, and she's tired a lot because she's taking care of a 1-year-old too. Last night she was a little irritated because I wasn't being as helpful as I could be. Instead of trying to come up with words to soothe and show my understanding, I quickly got my apron out and set about physically showing her that I empathize with her fatigue and irritation. Later she said she was sorry for being that way, to which I responded there is no need for apology.

When people act out toward us, it is up to us to create the situation we desire; not them. We can only control our own reactions; not others. I chose to take my wife's irritation, feel it, empathize and physically do something to show I care and understand.

I'll goof it up next time, but I am working toward being better. I am working toward being a person who listens and then acts. That's how you share your care.

4. What have been the consequences of your ability to share? Will that experience influence your future decisions to share?

The consequences have been everything in my life. All good comes from sharing. If you have good in your life, you have shared.

Additionally, taking the good you have received from sharing and then sharing that makes the world richer and more beautiful.

I shared a feeling one time, and now I have a beautiful family. Now I take the wonderful feelings they give me and share that with everyone I meet, whether it's a co-worker I see every day or a random person next to me on the train.

Kindness is a major consequence of sharing.

The future is only about sharing. If we stop sharing our empathy, we stop being human.

5. How have you been able to give to others while not overdoing it?

Hahaha. I overdo it sometimes. I also underdo it.

I try to err on the side of overdoing, whether it's telling my wife I love her, hugging a friend or crying at an emotional scene in a movie. Overdo it when you can, because when this life is over, you'll wish you did.

6. What advice would you give to others who will be reading this book so that they have a more fulfilling life of giving and caring for themselves and for others?

I am not qualified to give advice, but I have questions for the readers.

Without being morbid, consider your own death every day. When you are gone, what do you want people to remember you for? Consider your final living moments, whenever they may be. What will be important to you in those last few breaths?

Katie, College Student

1. How has your past influenced you to do what you are doing or what you have done?

Although maybe I couldn't say exactly why, I know that my past, my family, and my experiences strongly drive my decisions. There is a strong culture of individuality in the Western Hemisphere and a group mindset in Eastern thought. I believe that both are true. I am a product of my environment, but I also have the ability to grow in the directions that I want to grow in. I can embrace these experiences or react against them. For myself, I embrace my past from what it is - a cornerstone of how I think and feel about the world around me.

2. Is there anyone in the past and/or currently who has influenced you to be the sharing, caring kind of person who you are?

That is such a difficult question in so many ways. I think that you first have to answer a different question. Can someone be a caring, sharing, or kind person without someone else's positive influence? I would answer "No." I don't think it's possible, but that dovetails into existential questions about the nature of humankind: Are we naturally good or evil or is that just a construct we've created?

So, has someone influenced me to be the way I am? Absolutely. My parents, my teachers, my siblings, my friends, my God, etc. These people challenge me to be open and honest about who I am, how I feel, and if I need to adjust myself. As a kid I remember listening to audio lessons on effective conflict resolution and we talked a lot about personal character in my house. As a semi-adult, I still hold on to these ideas, seek advice from those who instilled those values in me, and surround myself with friends who push me to grow in how I treat others.

3. How have you been able to show that you care to share?

Again, that is such a complex answer. To me, sharing is Helped and difficult. It is about honesty and sacrifice. But how do I show that I want to share with others? I think that expressing genuine interest in others is where it starts. The key to sharing, I think, is listening. When someone listens and exhibits interest, they indicate aspects of their character. To my own mind, someone who is willing to actively listen, shows that they care to share.

4. What have been the consequences of your ability to share? Will that experience influence your future decisions to share?

Sharing, like I mentioned, has helped. You give your time, your interest, and, in the end, a part of yourself. There's always a danger of rejection or hurt, but in my own relationships, I have always found it worthwhile. In fact, I think these time-tested relationships I've developed through mutually sharing serve as an anchor. Because I have love and trust in these people, I feel more comfortable with expanding my vulnerability towards others. I care to share.

Better yet, I dare to share and take the risk with vulnerability and honesty because I know I can fall back on the love, acceptance, and respect that those close to me continually show. In a way, then, sharing has emboldened me.

5. How have you been able to give to others while not overdoing it?

Yes. Of course. However, I think that I fall into this imbalance when my motivation for sharing is self-oriented. If I share with others to be helpful, kind, etc., it's ineffective It's an exterior motive, and I think people can sense that. If my end goal is respect and love others, then sharing is important, but so is respecting the boundaries and desires of those I'm interacting with. In the same way, though, if I share completely exclusive to my own wants or needs, that isn't constructive either.

To make a vague answer slightly less ambiguous: I think that I have been relatively successful, but that balance ultimately requires a special self awareness and sensitivity to others.

6. What advice would you give to others who will be reading this book so that they have a more fulfilling life of giving and caring for themselves and for others?

I believe that we were created for a purpose and should rely on God for our strength, but whatever your background, fulfillment is gained out of sacrifice, sharing, and giving. But! You *absolutely* cannot give out of emptiness. Take care of yourself and recognize where your current path is going. Life is not a sprint, it's a marathon. So, ask yourself hard questions: "Where will my current path take me in X years? And do I want that?"

In the end, I believe that no one can do anything on their own. So yes! Share. But receive. But most importantly, do it with humility - not thinking less of yourself, but thinking about yourself less.

Salima - A Businesswoman

1. How has your past influenced you to do what you are doing or what you have done?

Seven to eight years ago, I was constantly in search of something bigger than me. I was

dreaming big and spending so much time chasing my dreams that were supposed to come true one day. Until one day a friend suggested to read Robin Sharma's world's bestseller "The Monk Who Sold His Ferrari". I was so impressed by the book that under its spell I decided to look at my own life. So, I put the timeline of my life down on paper which I did. Usually the life line should have Past, Present and Future. Mine had only Future. When asked why, I realized few important things:

A. Past never bothered me much, I was not carrying it as an old suitcase, which is by itself a great state of mind;
B. I never managed to focus on the Present as I believed that there was always a better place to be ("place" means state of

mind but location);

C. I wanted to plan, sketch and color my Future as I believed that it will be better than The Now.

This was the way my life line was structured. Nothing but Future. The basic straight-line

that I draw on a piece of paper help me to understand 3 key facts about myself:

- Life unfolds in the Present and Future hinges my ability to pay attention to the Now, to be in The Now;

- Future is a hiding place for people who are unsatisfied with their Now and I decided to find out what was wrong with my Now;

- For me the most important relationship is my relationship with myself which sets the base for my relationships with others.

Today I live my life based on these core values I set and honestly now the present seems quite satisfactorily and a pleasant place to be.

2. Is there anyone in the past and/or currently who has influenced you to be the caring, sharing kind of person who you are?

My parents gave me a solid foundation to start an independent journey in life. In addition to them I am fortunate to have a very dear person in my life who became an unofficial life coach for me. He helped me to see the best in me, to gain my confidence back, to believe in myself and have faith in people around me. He taught me not to judge, helped me to be able to think out of the box and to love people unconditionally without any expectations.

With [my life coach's help], I finally understood that if I love myself, I will love people; that I'm very blessed and gifted to be loved by so many extraordinary people I've surrounded myself with. Even though sometimes I call myself "a pleaser" I know that it derives from my desire to make people happy, to be responsible at least for a little smile on someone's face.

3. How have you been able to show that you care to share?

I believe in a power of self. There is nothing as powerful as a human being. It's up to us to turn the power we possess, either to good or bad. We quite often complain that people don't understand us. Recently I caught myself claiming that: "he never knew who I was". This thought disturbed me for a while until I asked myself: Did I show him my true self? The answer was negative. People know us as much as we want them to know, so, yes, now I'm dedicated to show that I care to share myself. Because it will make my relationships stronger and well balanced without any blame game.

4. What have been the consequences of your ability to share?

Will that experience influence your future decisions to share? – Sharing or not sharing can have both good and bad consequences. A real story that happened to me when I was 20. Late afternoon in February on my way to the dentist I got into the bakery and left it with few cold sandwiches in a rush. With the corner of my eye I noticed a very old woman who asked to share a food with her. I was so much in rush that decided to ignore her and passed by quickly.

After 10 minutes I got hit by the car on the same road, ended up in a hospital with severe injuries. When I opened my eyes in a hospital a day later, I vividly remember seeing that old woman's face leaning over me.

I immediately shut my eyes trying to remember who she was and I immediately knew the answer. It was a lady whom I decided to ignore. Pulled all my will together and opened eye again. This time it was my mom by my bedside. When I asked, they said there was no old woman in my room, just mom and I. I instantly knew where I made a mistake. After 2 months when I was able to walk, I started to look for that old woman. As if she disappeared, there wasn't any trace of hers. Finally, I gave up. A year passed until once I saw her sitting at the same spot again. I sat next to her. She didn't even look at me. I asked if she remembered me.

The answer was No. I showed her my still remaining bruises and told her my story. She raised her eyes and said "Sorry". Of course, I know that she personally didn't do anything to me, it was my choice to be careless, rude, ignorant. I got to the same store, got her some sandwiches and water. Handed it to her. When I said her Thank you for a life lesson to my surprise she said: "You are welcome" ... Now I don't want to interpret this occurrence as something extraordinary, but if to look at the core of the story ability to share is given to every human being. The point is to be able to use it to do good and help others.

5. How have you been able to give to others while not overdoing it?

I strongly believe in the value of sharing which can be applied to anything from love, kindness, inspiration, passion, or even tangible monetary values. I'm sure everyone at least once in their life time says: I will give to the one who knows how to give back. Even if it seems like everything is mutual, on a two-way street called life, it's very common to end up alone. Does that mean we should lose faith in people, that we should stop caring just because something in the past went not as desired, that someone in the past didn't appreciate what we did? I don't think so.

I personally have a strong principle which is I will not let any bad experience to shape my attitude toward people. And since I'm a great pleaser, I know there always will be someone who will take advantage of me. I do realize that moderation is the key and over giving can destroy me as the person who I am today.

1. What advice would you give to others who will be reading this book so that they have a more fulfilling life of giving and caring for themselves and for others?

It's very important to be able to get out of our comfort zone, to put ourselves into others' shoes and then draw conclusions. I strongly believe that any communication is contagious. Considering that everyone wants to be treated well, we need to treat others well first. Only by understanding others it's possible to become a caring person.

Tim - Elementary School Teacher

1. How has your past influenced you to do what you are doing or what you have done?

My mother and aunt were outstanding teachers. I also had many excellent teachers in my childhood. David Strait and Martha Lund (Patton) at Sequoia school, and Bob Camden and Joe Handy at Manteca High were particularly influential to me. Great teachers like that make you want to become one yourself.

2. Is there anyone in the past and/or currently who have influenced you to be the sharing, caring kind of person who you are?

My mother, grandmother, and uncle Raymond were tremendous examples for me. My mother, Ruth Lewis, was a kindergarten teacher at French Camp School. She was the kind of teacher who always went the extra mile for her students. She would bring food and clothing to kids who had none, and she would bring kids from Mary Graham Hall home at Christmas when they had nowhere else to go. My grandmother cared for my invalid uncle Raymond on her own for many years. When I was old enough, I helped too. Even they would go out of their way to visit and bring gifts to people in convalescent hospitals.

Very early on, through all these people, I learned the value of giving to others and the joy that comes from that. I learned long ago that when I focused on myself and trying to make myself happy, I ended up miserable. When I focused on doing things for others, I would be happier in the end.

3. How have you been able to show that you care to share?

I am a 7/8 grade social studies teacher. The connection that I have with my students has always been based on the fact that I take the time and make the effort to be there for them. I spend a huge amount of time and effort not just teaching them, but going to their games and concerts, and showing them that I care about them. I speak to them with respect and I ask them their opinions and listen to their answers. I show them that I care about what they think, and that their thoughts are important. I go the extra mile to make things special and meaningful for them.

4. What have been the consequences of your ability to share?

I have been able to touch the lives of generations of children in my school's community. I have now taught many children of former students. I've seen many former students grow and blossom in many successful ways. Some are now doctors, dentists, lawyers, college professors, and dozens of teachers. Many have become successful in the entertainment industry, music, politics, and many other things. Many former students tell me that my classes changed their lives, or changed their perspectives on the world. I frequently get calls, letters, and emails from former students thanking me for what I've done for them. Many come back to visit me.

Please relationships mean the world to me. I've received a few awards and commendations, but I don't do what I do for my bosses, colleagues, or even the parents of my students. I'm there for the children, they know it, and I find that incredibly fulfilling.

5. How have you been able to give to others while not overdoing it?

You can't give to others who are not ready to accept your gift. Students don't always appreciate where I'm coming from or what I'm trying to do for them at first. A lot of it comes down to patience and persistence. You have to choose your spots, choose your battles. You have to go into each day with an open heart and you have to be a good listener. If you listen carefully, people will tell you what it is that they need. True caring isn't about giving people what you want them to have. It's about understanding what they truly need, and then helping them find it for themselves.

6. What advice would you give to others who will be reading this book so that they have a more fulfilling life of giving and caring for themselves and for others?

When you're truly focused on helping others, you have less time to worry about your own problems. You have less time to think about your own pain. And when you spend your time giving to others, you always end up getting as much or more back. Those are the things that truly make us happy, that make us feel whole. And those are the things that will cure whatever is ailing you, that will help to heal your own wounds. You have to take care of yourself so that you are available for others, but, in the long run, it is your caring for others that will bring real peace and happiness to your life.

Karen

1. How has your past influenced you to do what you are doing or what you have done? (No answer given.)

2. Is there anyone in the past and/or currently who has influenced you to be the sharing, caring kind of person who you are?

My past has everything to do with who I am and what I am doing. As long as I can remember, I have been surrounded by illness. My mother was the most inspirational person in my life. Her life on the outside, appeared as if it were perfect. But it was a life of physical pain, which drained her emotionally. My mother never complained, never felt as if she was cheated in life, and always had time for others, regardless of her circumstances. She was the most giving, selfless, and beautiful human being I have ever met.

It is because of her, I am who I am! She taught me to love deeply, genuinely, and to give freely!

Later in her life, she also faced a form of dementia called Cerebral Amyloid Angiopathy. This may have stripped her of her memory, but it never touched the love she had in her heart.

I witnessed the depth of her love. Words at times were not spoken, but it was in her touch, her smile, and her eyes. She was still Mom, and she continued to inspire me until the end.

3. How have you been able to show that you care to share?

(No answer given.)

4. What have been the consequences of your ability to share? Will that experience influence your future decisions to share?

Having both parents pass from dementia and Alzheimer's at a relatively young age, I knew I had to do my part to use my pain, my years of experience, to help others who find themselves traveling this same difficult path. I spend time supporting those who are new to this disease, and others who are at that point of exhaustion that comes with caring for people with this disease.

I also have a special place in my heart for the aging. So many reach this stage in life, and don't feel they have a purpose any longer. I have had events for special people in my life that have impacted so many over the years. I feel it's important that they continue to know their significance.

The outcome of these events has encouraged me to continue touching lives.

5. How have you been able to give to others while not overdoing it?

One issue I have is not overdoing it, in the process of helping others. It's hard for me to take a step back, but I am slowly learning to do so.

6. What advice would you give to others who will be reading this book so that they have a more fulfilling life of giving and caring for themselves and for others?

The only advice I can give for a more fulfilling life is to love deeply, love genuinely, and

give freely! My mother was one smart lady, and I miss her dearly!
Matthew - A Special Education Adult

1. How has your past influenced you to do what you are doing or what you have done?

My parents were hardworking and loving. The special education teachers helped me to be

a better person by being very kind to me and to others.

1. Is there anyone in the past and/or currently who has influenced you to be the sharing, caring kind of person who you are?

My special education teachers, my doctors, and my neighbors have influenced me to be

the sharing, caring kind of person who I am.

1. How have you been able to show that you care to share?

I love to volunteer and to donate my time at homeless shelters and at the dog pound.

1. What have been the consequences of your ability to share? Will that experience influence your future decisions to share?

Others have shown their appreciation. Others wish to be like he is.

1. How have you been able to give to others while not
    overdoing it?

I love helping others, although there are some people that
can't accept it well.

1. What advice would you give to others who will be reading
    this book so that they have a more fulfilling life of giving and
    caring for themselves and for others?

Listen more. Express kindness by saying "hi", "thank you",
and "have a great day!"

Anh - Orthopedic Surgeon

1. How has your past influenced you to do what you are doing
    or what you have done?

I was a boat refugee and saw a lot of suffering. Now, I am
providing comfort.

1. Is there anyone in the past and/or currently who has
    influenced you to be the sharing, caring kind of person who
    you are?

My father was a surgeon. His professionalism was very
helpful for me.

1. How have you been able to show that you care to share?

I have displayed caring and sharing through actions and by
compassions of all

walks of life.

1. What have been the consequences of your ability to share?
    Will that experience influence your future decisions to share?

I have been able to teach along with being a doctor.

1. How have you been able to give to others while not
    overdoing it?

I have cut down in my professional responsibilities.

1. What advice would you give to others who will be reading
    this book so that they have a more fulfilling life of giving and
    caring for themselves and for others?

Everybody needs to love what they are doing in order to be
happy.

Kory, a pharmacist technician

1. How has your past influenced you to do what you are doing
    or what you have done?

When I was 16, my Dad passed away from cancer. Those
who helped him made me

want to help others.

1. Is there anyone in the past and/or currently who has
    influenced you to be the sharing, caring kind of person who
    you are?

My parents

1. How have you been able to show that you care to share?

Through my work and going the extra mile, paying attention to details.

1. What have been the consequences of your ability to share? Will that experience influence your future decisions to share?

Sometimes, it takes away time from my own family, but they are understanding.

1. How have you been able to give to others while not overdoing it?

You have to identify your own limitations and boundaries so you don't get burnt out.

1. What advice would you give to others who will be reading this book so that they have a more fulfilling life of giving and caring for themselves and for others?

Caring is the best way to give back. Ultimately, I believe we are here to serve each other!

Jayne, a caregiver

1. How has your past influenced you to do what you are doing or what you have done?

She grew up with elderly parents around. Her parents had a foster child. Parents were

calm. She has a lot of respect for the elderly.

1. Is there anyone in the past and/or currently who has influenced you to be the sharing, caring kind of person who you are?

Her foster parents.

1. How have you been able to show that you care to share?

She shows that she cares and shares by showing respect, listening to the elderly, and

going above and beyond the normal caregiver responsibilities.

1. What have been the consequences of your ability to share? Will that experience influence your future decisions to share?

The caregiver becomes a family member.

1. How have you been able to give to others while not overdoing it?

It is hard to do. She needs more downtime by being involved with athletics, family,

and friends.

1. What advice would you give to others who will be reading this book so that they have a more fulfilling life of giving and caring for themselves and for others?

Be more loving to your family. Be compassionate.
Rita, Community Engagement Manager, Global Public Affairs
1. How has your past influenced you to do what you are doing or what you have done?
My first experience with service to others was when I was a junior usher at Sweet Home Baptist Church, Kentwood, LA. Grandmother asked if I wanted to help out, and she launched a lifelong commitment to giving back to others.

2. Is there anyone in the past and/or currently who has influenced you to be the caring, sharing kind of person who you are?

Modie Holiday, my paternal grandmother.

3. How have you been able to show that you care to share?

My career at Intel is about encouraging and inspiring our employees to volunteer/give back to the community?

Serving as a Commissioner for the State of California Volunteers, appointed by Arnold Schwarzenegger, and re-appointed by Gov. Jerry Brown.

Serving on the Board of Directors for the Mission City Community Fund, City of Santa Clara

Served on the Historic Commission, City of Santa Clara,

Served on the Sports Commission, City of Stockton

Served on the Human Rights Commission, City of San Jose

Served on the YWCA Silicon Valley Board of Directors

Served as co-chair & Chair of The Corporate Community Relations Consortium, Bay Area

4. What have been the consequences of your ability to share? Will that experience influence future decisions to share?

I have not experienced any consequences.

5. How have you been able to give to others while not overdoing it?

As I was growing my career at Intel in the philanthropy space, it was difficult to balance saying no to the numerous worthy causes seeking my skills on their boards or advisory councils.

6. What advice would you give to others who will be reading this book so that they have a more fulfilling life of giving and caring for themselves and for others?

Volunteering/Serving is something that everyone can do. If you are new to a neighborhood, city, state, country, volunteering seems to be the best way to get to know people, and learn about your new environment, well at least it has been that for me.

Jeff, Founder and Director for charity that provides musical instruments to low income schools

1. How has your past influenced you to do what you are doing or what you have done?

Throughout my life I have experienced the power of music on many different levels. These experiences lead me to begin Hungry for Music's outreach. Even though I am not a musician myself, I experienced music's power to connect, inspire, motivate, and heal. Being aware of this power, I want Hungry for Music to reach as many young musicians as possible.

2. Is there anyone in the past and/or currently who has influenced you to be the caring, sharing kind of person who you are?

My mom, godmother, and a caretaker when I was younger all showed me the importance of helping others that are less fortunate as a way of dealing with our own pain. We transcend our pain, when we help others.

3. How have you been able to show that you care to share?

Through how I live my life on a daily basis and through HFM's outreach.

4. What have been the consequences of your ability to share? Will that experience influence future decisions to share?

It comes back. Our outreach grows and grows. But I try not to think about it. I just do it, knowing it's the right thing. The way I see it. We are here to help others. To share our strength.

5. How have you been able to give to others while not overdoing it?

It's a fine line. I definitely have to remind myself that I have needs that need tending and to take time for myself.

6. What advice would you give to others who will be reading this book so that they have a more fulfilling life of giving and caring for themselves and for others?

If you feel compelled to give. Do. Listen to that intuitive nudge. Don't overextend yourself and don't have any expectations. Just do it.

We wish to thank the people who took the time to reflect on and to answer the above six questions related to their lives so that you can become inspired by them as well. It has been an honor to care and to share their ideas.

Rex Holiday, Summer Hornstein, Steve Sonntag, many other people, and organizations are some of the many messengers of ideas and hope, so that your lives and the people around you can be that much happier and that much more fulfilled. Our current global crisis, while it has sadly taken many lives and created a lot of emotional and financial stress, does not define us. We do, by how we treat ourselves and how we treat one another.

Suggested Resources

BOOKS

Gibranb, Kahlil. *The Prophet.* Hertfordshire, England: Wordsworth Editions, Limited, 1997.

Gomez, German. *Write It Down: The Edge That Can Make You Stand Out.*

Korgan, Grant. *Two Feet Back.* Carson City, NV: Lucky Bat Books, 2012.

Reeve, Christopher. *Nothing Is Impossible.* New York: Random House, 2002.

Stock, Gregory. *The Book Of Questions.* New York: Workman, 1987.

Stock, Gregory. *The Kids' Book Of Questions.* New York: Workman, 2004.

PERIODICALS, MAGAZINE ARTICLES, JOURNAL ARTICLES & ONLINE JOURNALS

Cameron, Laurie P. 2018. The Power of Mindfulness and Compassion. Greenbranch Publication,

LLC, 251-253.

Devor, Marshall, Rappaport, Isabelle & Rappaport, Z. Harry. 2015. Does the Golem Feel Pain?

Moral Instincts and Ethical Dilemmas Concerning Suffering and the Brain. *World Institute of*

Pain: Pain Practice, 15(6), 497-508.

Friedman, Hershey H. & Gerstein, Miriam. 2017. Leading With Compassion: The Key to Changing the Organizational Culture and Achieving Success. *Psychosociological Issues in*

Human Resource Management 5(1), 160-175.

Leaviss, J. & Uttley, L. 2014. Psychotherapeutic Benefits of Compassion-Focused Therapy: An

Early Systematic Review. *Psychological Medicine* 45, 927-945.

Levine, Daniel S. 2017. Modeling the Instinctive-Emotional-Thoughtful Mind. *Cognitive*

Systems Research 45, 82-94.

Seppala, Emma M. 2013. Compassion: Our First Instinct. *Psychology Today.* Retrieved

April 1, 2018:

https://www.psychologytoday.com/us/blog/feeling-it/201306/compassion-our-first-instinct.

Widlok, Thomas. 2013. Allowing Others to Take What Is Valued. *HAU: Journal of*

Ethnographic Theory 3 (2), 11-31.

Zaki, Jamil, 2009. The Altruism Instinct. *Psychology Today.* Retrieved April 1, 2018;

https://www.psychologytoday.com/us/blog/your-brain-us/200911/the-altruism-instinct

MOVIES

O'Toole, Peter, Sophia Loren, James Coco. *Man of La Mancha,* DVD, Directed by Arthur Hiller,

Los Angeles: Shout Factory, 2017.

Robins, Barry, Miles Chapin, Darel Glaser. *Bless the Beasts and Children,* DVD, Directed by

Stanley Kramer, Culver City, CA, Sony Pictures Home, 1971.

WEBSITES

American Civil Liberties Union. www.aclu.org[1].

American Federation of Teachers. www.aft.org[2].

Ask Me Anything. www.amafeed.com[3].

Be The Match. www.bethematch.org[4].

---

1.   http://www.aclu.org

2.   http://www.aft.org

3.   http://www.amafeed.com

4.   http://www.bethematch.org

Biography (Patti Hearst): www.biography.com/people/patti-hearst-9332960[5].

Chicken Soup for the Soul. www.chickensoup.com[6].

CNN. www.cnn.com[7].

Curriki. www.curriki.org[8].

Doctors Without Borders. www.doctorswithoutborders.org[9].

Dr. Wayne Dyer. www.drwaynedyer.com[10].

Easter Seals. www.easterseals.com[11].

FaceTime. www.facetime.com[12].

Free Rice. www.freerice.com[13].

Future Teachers of America. www.futureteachers.org[14].

The Gates Scholarship. www.thegatesscholarship.org[15].

Global Giving. www.globalgiving.org[16].

Go Fund Me. www.gofundme.com[17].

Goodwill Industries International, Inc. www.goodwill.org[18].

Google Classroom. www.edu.google.com[19].

Dr. Louise Hay. www.louisehay.com[20].

---

5.   http://www.biography.com/people/patti-hearst-9332960

6.   http://www.chickensoup.com

7.   http://www.cnn.com

8.   http://www.curriki.org

9.   http://www.doctorswithoutborders.org

10.   http://www.drwaynedyer.com

11.   http://www.easterseals.com

12.   http://www.facetime.com

13.   http://www.freerice.com

14.   http://www.futureteachers.org

15.   http://www.thegatesscholarship.org

16.   http://www.globalgiving.org

17.   http://www.gofundme.com

18.   http://www.goodwill.org

19.   http://www.edu.google.com

Help A Reporter. www.helpareporter.com[21].

Hospice. www.hospicefoundation.org[22].

I Can Help. www.icanhelpdeletenegativity.org[23].

The Innocence Project. www.innoncenceproject.org[24].

iHeartRadio. www.iheart.com[25].

JustServe. www.justserve.org[26].

Latin Dictionary. www.latin-dictionary.net[27].

Loving Healing Press Books. www.lovinghealing.com[28].

The Ronald McDonald House. www.rmhc.org[29].

Make-A-Wish. www.wish.org[30].

Mentoring. www.mentoring.org[31].

Merriam Webster (Oedipus Complex). www.merriam-webster.com/dictionary/Oedipus%20 complex.

Myofascial Release Therapy. www.myofascialrelease.com[32].

National Association for the Advancement of Colored People. www.naacp.org[33].

National Educators Association. www.nea.org[34].

---

20.   http://www.louisehay.com

21.   http://www.helpareporter.com

22.   http://www.hospicefoundation.org

23.   http://www.icanhelpdeletenegativity.org

24.   http://www.innoncenceproject.org

25.   http://www.iheart.com

26.   http://www.justserve.org

27.   http://www.latin-dictionary.net

28.   http://www.lovinghealing.com

29.   http://www.rmhc.org

30.   http://www.wish.org

31.   http://www.mentoring.org

32.   http://www.myofascialrelease.com

33.   http://www.naacp.org

34.   http://www.nea.org

National Parent Teacher Association. www.pta.org[35].

National Public Radio. www.npr.org[36].

Oprah Winfrey. www.oprah.com[37].

Red Cross. www.redcross.org[38].

Fred Rogers. www.pbskids.org/rogers[39].

St. Jude's Hospital. www.stjude.org[40].

Salvation Army. www.salvationarmyusa.org[41].

Sesame Street. www.pbskids.org/sesame[42].

Shriners Hospital. www.shrinershospitalsforchildren.org/shc[43].

Skype. www.skype.com[44].

Smithsonian.com (Stockholm Syndrome). www.smithsonianmag.com/smart-new/six-day-hostage-standoff-gave-rise-stockholm-syndrome-180964537[45].

Society for the Prevention of Cruelty to Animals. www.spcai.org[46].

Southern Poverty Law Center. www.splcenter.org[47].

Special Olympics. www.specialolympics.org[48].

Teachers Pay Teachers. www.teacherspayteachers.com[49].

---

35.   http://www.pta.org

36.   http://www.npr.org

37.   http://www.oprah.com

38.   http://www.redcross.org

39.   http://www.pbskids.org/rogers

40.   http://www.stjude.org

41.   http://www.salvationarmyusa.org

42.   http://www.pbskids.org/sesame

43.   http://www.shrinershospitalsforchildren.org/shc

44.   http://www.skype.com

45.   http://www.smithsonianmag.com/smart-new/six-day-hostage-standoff-gave-rise-stockholm-syndrome-180964537

46.   http://www.spcai.org

47.   http://www.splcenter.org

48.   http://www.specialolympics.org

Teachers Without Borders. www.teacherswithoutborders.org[50].

TED. www.ted.com[51].

UNICEF. www.unicefusa.org[52].

United Way. www.unitedway.org[53].

Wikipedia. www.wikipedia.org[54].

Writer's Market. www.writersmarket.com[55].

WyzAnt. www.wyzant.com[56].

You Tube. www.youtube.com[57].

Zoom. www.zoom.us[58].

---

49.   http://www.teacherspayteachers.com

50.   http://www.teacherswithoutborders.org

51.   http://www.ted.com

52.   http://www.unicefusa.org

53.   http://www.unitedway.org

54.   http://www.wikipedia.org

55.   http://www.writersmarket.com

56.   http://www.wyzant.com

57.   http://www.youtube.com

58.   http://www.zoom.us

About The Authors

Dr. Rex Allen Holiday earned his doctorate in educational leadership with an emphasis in e-learning, and his professional interests are STEM research, curriculum development, instructional design, critical thinking theory, and quantitative reasoning. He is a part-time professor, wireless engineering consultant, peer reviewer, editor, National Science Foundation review panelist, and former school board trustee.

Summer Horenstein is a graduate from Brigham Young University living in Utah with her husband and four children. She enjoys volunteering in her community: including working with the Cub Scouts and the local elementary school. She also has taken her passion for music and sports to coordinating and hosting such events as a monthly Music and Story time for young children and a non-competitive amateur Sports Night for Women.

Steve Sonntag has been a mentor teacher, his district's high school teacher of the year, a language chairperson, a tutor, a workshop presenter, a participant in high school accreditations, and an author during the past forty-nine years. He emphasizes and practices insight, hope, and inspiration to students, families, and teachers.

www.ingramcontent.com/pod-product-compliance
Lightning Source LLC
Chambersburg PA
CBHW051228160726
47994CB00002B/798